The Ou Handbook

How To Be A Modern Outlaw & Gain

Freedom In An Unfree World

Charles Sledge

Copyright © 2017 Charles Sledge

All rights reserved.

I am not a doctor. My books do not contain medical advice. All contents of my books are for informational, educational, and for entertainment purposes only. Reliance on any information of charlessledge.com & any books written by Charles Sledge is solely at your own risk. No liability will be assumed for the use of any information provided or contributed in my books. Consult a professional before following any of my advice.

Table Of Contents

Table Of Contents

Introduction

The Slave Morality

The Outlaw Takes What He Wills

The Outlaw & Respect

An Outlaw's Loyalty

The Outlaw Plays To Win

The Duality Of An Outlaw

An Understanding Of The World Unknown To Most

The Outlaw's Unique Path

Snakes & Wolves

Gaining Freedom In An Unfree World

About The Author

Introduction

Do you feel free?

My guess is that if you're an average man living in the Western world that you don't. Your source of enslavement or limitation may feel like it comes from many different directions and many different ways. And you'd be right.

From a corporate job and a sadistic boss killing your soul to a nagging wife nipping at your balls to a media that has all but declared outright war on you and what you are.

Playing by the old rules is a guaranteed way to slavery. Playing by their rules is a guaranteed way to enslavement as a matter of fact playing by any other rules than your own isn't going to get you where you want…to freedom.

Here I declare the man in order to reclaim his freedom and be what he was created to be must throw off the yoke of slavery and dogma passed down to him by his masters. And instead must live in accordance with what is best for himself and his freedom.

To be a modern outlaw and find freedom in an increasingly unfree and regulated world. A world that is on the path to eliminating all risk and along with it masculinity. An environment that wishes to cage you in and say it's for your benefit. An environment without glory, honor, or growth. A sickening neutered unnatural state. But my guess is if you're reading this book that you have no interest in being part of that movement.

You want to rebel against it, to fight against what is coming. Like I said to be an outlaw. Perhaps the idea of being an outlaw gives you a bad feeling, it shouldn't. In corrupt times to upright are the outlaws. In an upside down world good is considered bad and bad good. And friend we live in an upside down world.

To be a "bad" man by society should be worn as a badge of honor. As should the declaration that you are an outlaw. You are outside this society of decay and degeneracy and wish for something stronger and more true. Something that isn't found in an cage but rather is found out there.

In the wilds where the outlaw ride. If that is where you feel your destiny lies than this book is for you. It will teach you the ways of the outlaw and how to begin to gain freedom for yourself. It is meant to break the chains of both your spirit and mind and rekindle the fire that burns deep down within all of us.

Now get ready to learn what it takes to make it into the ranks of free rebels, of men without masters, of outlaws.

The Slave Morality

Ever got the feeling that your mind is not your own? Have you ever wondered why you do the things that you do? Why is it that man behaves in a certain way even though it is against his best interest? Truth be told most of us are living in a zombified state. Our minds and our hearts are not our own but rather a mix of programming and brainwashing designed to get us to act and behave in a certain way. A certain way that was never made for our own benefit but rather for the benefit of those who instilled these notions into our head. For example you may think that there is a nobleness in sorts of allowing someone to take advantage of you without retaliation. Why is this? Certainly this is not something that man was born with (otherwise he'd be extinct).

This docile, passive, and weak nature is something that is fostered in man and all is done to make sure that nothing comes in and breaks it. Those that are truly free and truly men, the outlaws, barbarians, or whatever you want to call them are deemed evil, awful, a whole list of "ist"'s and "phobes" and every other shaming word that they can come up with. When all they really are is freedom and a way to break free from the plantation. However we obviously can't have that so freedom is labeled evil, up down, and good evil. And the matrix continues on, the drones dying out and being replaced by new ones. An endless soulless cycle that we are supposed to not only cherish and be thankful for but to defend and uphold.

We are conditioned to be slaves. Anyone who questions this slave morality is deemed a heretic or evil. This is nothing new, truth be told the mass of humanity has always lived as a servant class of some sort. And the mass of humanity will always be a servant class of some sort. This isn't to cast hate on them or anything of that matter, simply a statement of facts. However there are also other sides of humanity. There are the slave masters who wish to run the slaves lives and have them do as they want to make their own lives easier. Then there are the outlaws who wish to go their own way and experience the freedom, trial, and challenge of the world on their own. They have no need of slaves and certainly no need of slave masters.

Breaking Free

However to become an outlaw and be free first one must loosen the chains that bind him. Loosen and weaken them until with a mighty pull they can be snapped and the beginnings of freedom achieved. Most men will never know what this feels like both the thrill and anxiety of having freedom before their eyes and within their grasp. The first step is to be aware that many of your thoughts are not your own by rather put there by those who do not have your best interest at heart and want you to be a docile slave that they can do as they please with. Some will be treated half way decently and maybe even thrown a bone every now and then while others will be beaten and bruised with glee as their masters laugh because they know there is nothing they can do.

Much better is the fate of the outlaw, the free man who holds his fate in his own hand. Sure he will never experience the comfort of the plantation but he will experience so much more. So many more things greater and of higher worth. And this all starts with taking measure of one's thoughts and beliefs. When you sit back and you look at things and you ask yourself "does this benefit me or someone else?" you find that many beliefs and ideas that you have been grasping onto are the very chains that keep you bound. This isn't to say that every belief you've ever had is wrong. Rather that some of your more prized and cherished ones may not be yours at all or for your benefit.

Regardless you'll only learn this by examining yourself and your beliefs. Question things and see what the logical conclusion is. The actions that you take are they actions that actually benefit you? Or rather are they actions that you do because others told you to do them, it's what everyone does, or one of the most popular "it's the right thing to do". The right thing to do according to who? And does this person who is telling you it is the right thing to do have your best interests at heart? Unless it's a strong father, mentor, or brother my guess is going to be no. And therefore if the belief has no use for you then discard it.

The Making Of A Slave

From an early age we are taught how to behave. In a natural society this is generally a good thing and even in our society now we are taught many good things. The basics of socializing and things of that nature. However we're also taught many things that are designed to make up complacent and to ensure that we never question our chains or grow angry at them. We are often discouraged from questioning certain things or believing certain thoughts. At first we may fight this but then eventually we generally give in, on the strongest will carry this independent thought into adult hood. That's not to say that everything that's not mainstream is good or that everything mainstream is bad. This concept can be taken too far and many times is. But it is something to think about.

A slave is made when one gives up their self-determination. When they accept whatever is placed before them and refuse to ever question if it's what should be placed before them or the whole story. The slave lives in a dream world, though it may be a pleasant one to the slave. The outlaw, the man, lives in the real world and all that entails. It's not very pretty, it's actually pretty damn ugly. But it's true and it basing your beliefs and mind on these truths that makes you free. You must follow a code that reflects your own values and that is there for your own benefit. You must get rid of the chains that are put upon you by others, the slave morality.

Every outlaw has their code and their code differs from the slave morality of mainstream society as a whole. A man cannot live without something which to base and measure his conduct. This code should be something developed to make you sharp and hold you to a high level. It should be something that is not easy to hold yourself to and that requires challenges and sacrifice. It should emphasize strength and overcoming challenge. Have your own moral system that is first and foremost designed for your benefit not for the benefit of humanity as a whole (a nebulous term) nor for others and especially not for those who would use you as a pawn to be sacrificed and discarded when the time comes. Your code must benefit you first and foremost, that is the only type of code worth following.

The Outlaw Takes What He Wills

You've been told ever since you were young to ask for permission. While there is certainly a time and place for this (when young and among elders within your tribe) following this same line of thought in the real world will get you killed. Imagine being a hunter who asked for the prey's permission to hunt and kill it. That hunter would be extinct as well as all he provided for. Or imagine that you asked for your enemies permission to retaliate against an attack they made against you. You'd be a fool and just like our hunter quickly go extinct. In this world you take what you can, you take what you can through your strength. Victory is often pried from the cold dead hands of your enemies, it is not something that is given to you freely.

The outlaw takes what he wills from the world. Like the conqueror he knows there is a rich bounty for those that have the strength to claim it. So he takes what he can for himself. He isn't laden down with guilt from a slave morality he knows that to eat he must kill and to survive he must fight. He has no illusions about how the world works and who comes out on top. The outlaw sees what is around him as his domain or domain to be conquered. The outlaw knows that the strongest take what they will and everyone else deals with it. Strength rules the day in the outlaw's world and he takes account of this. Always testing and observing the strength of others while constantly refining his own strength.

While there is a time and place for fairness within one's own group and for competitive purposes when it comes to claiming and acquiring resources (whatever those resources may be) those who follow fairness (as however their tribe defines it) are destined to lose. For in the real world the only thing that matters is victory not the means by which victory is achieved. This doesn't mean you have to be amoral, deceitful, and what one would call "evil" to succeed. One can be both wise and strong without those things yet to pretend they won't be used or that they don't exist is foolishness. The outlaw expects his enemy and competitors to use every dirty underhand trick in the book and then some to achieve their ends. The outlaw is ready for this and ready to respond in kind.

A World For The Taking

The spoils go to the victor. Those who take what they will get what they want. It's as simple as that. Those that sit back and wait for providence, fairness, or something else to achieve there ends for them will be waiting for eternity and will never get what they want. You only eat what you kill. The world is ripe for plunderer's strong enough to take it's bounty. The world has always gone to the strongest conquerors and it always will. While things like rules and fairness are used to bar others from the competition. Look at it this way. Imagine you hadn't eaten for days and there a hundred feet away was a wounded animal lying still fresh killed and there one hundred feet past that was another man also looking starving.

Now imagine you could tell that man "We will fight but you should only use one hand" and that he actually followed it. You would laugh as you ate the wounded animal over his corpse. You would laugh because you couldn't believe that a man could be so foolish and yet he was. That is what it's like competing in the world adhering to a code that is not for your own interest. It's fight with one hand behind your back while everyone else is not only using both hands but also have brass knuckles. There is no such thing as a fair fight in the real world. There is only winner and loser. The outlaw understands this and does everything possible to ensure victory for himself and his gang.

He'll use any means necessarily as it is victory and survival that he is after. Not saying he lost "fairly". The outlaw also helps himself freely to the spoils of victory. He knows that what he wins is his so long as he is strong and quick enough to keep it. An outlaw is not a follower by nature. He is a leader even if he chooses to sometimes walk alone. He doesn't buy into false moralities but rather looks at the world and nature and rather sees what actually works and what actually causes one to achieve victory more often than not. That is where he draws his code from, from the harsh reality of existence. He cobbles it together from the coldness of the world.

The Will To Power

The outlaw is too wise to allow his enemies a chance to breath, mercy, or a second chance. If he has the chance to end them then he will regardless if it's considered "fair". Like I've said what the outlaw looks for is survival not dying for a false moral code that does nothing for him but keep him in chains. He asserts his dominance and strength without a second thought. He does not care what others think but rather what is good for him and will bring him the greatest victory in this world. He understands that those who have power are those that have taken it, often from others who would rather not relinquish it to him.

This doesn't mean that he is necessarily cruel though he can be, it means he is practical. The relationship between unapologetically asserting oneself and one's will is what brings a person what they want in this life. He knows that showing any sign of weakness to his enemies isn't the mark of a good man but the mark of a fool who will soon be eliminated. He looks around him and see that many suffer because of the chains that have inflicted on themselves and the "rules" they bring into combat where rules are meaningless. People are handicapped by their own self-restraint and sense of "fairness".

Which makes them easy pickings for the wolves. There are many matters in which exercising one's self-restraint can be good but when it comes to asserting oneself in this world then self-restraint can end your reign before it even started. You must go all in, there can be no half-measure. You cannot hold back hoping your enemy will not come at you with everything he has, because he will. He makes no apologies for taking what he wants and dares anyone to try and stop him or take it from him. Outlaws are controlled by their own code and what is best for them not by the shame and guilt of others. In this regard the outlaw is pragmatic and does what works not what sounds nice.

The Outlaw & Respect

Man chases after many different things in this world. Some chase money, some chase women, some chase comfort. Some are "successful" (as they get what they've been chasing) while others are not so successful and so keep themselves rushing forward trying to get after whatever it is they seek. Men seek these things because they believe it will give them what they want in life. They think if I get this thing then I will be good and all will be well. Of course as soon as man achieves what he strives after he is then unsatisfied with it and so the entire circle starts all over again. Sometimes to goal has changed and sometimes to goal is simply a bigger measure of the same thing they were chasing all along.

A bigger house, a blonder wife, a bigger bank account, a cushier position, and so on and so forth. Not realizing that ultimately these things are all vanity and not things that are going to give man what he seeks. The outlaw because of his harsher upbringing closer to reality understands this and seeks the one currency that never depreciates and that all take notice of no matter their race, creed, or religion. And that is respect. Above all else the outlaw seeks that others respect him. He does not care if he is liked nor if he is in the "right" (often according to slave morality anyways) rather he only cares if his strength is respected. If the respect is there then all is good, if it's not well then we have a problem.

Respect is the ultimate currency in which the outlaw trades and which matters most to him. Sure he will pursue money and women have a place in his life. But they do not occupy the central part, no the central part is occupied by respect. He can lose money and it means little, lose women and it means even less. But lose respect and it must be fixed immediately. Because with loss of respect comes many other negative things. Without respect there is not much that a man has in this world. As you'll see a man's sense of masculinity and that respect that is given to him have a nearly direct correlation with one another. That is granted that the respect is coming from other strong men especially within the gang who hold to the same honor system as he does.

The Source Of Respect

Respect comes from a man's strength plain and simple. A man who isn't strong isn't going to be respected. He may be "good", he may be moral, and he may be a "pillar of the community" but he will not be respected. Sure he'll get the plastic "respect" of those around him. The babbling masses but as soon as something goes wrong they'd turn on him and tear him down in a second. The respect like the bond with fair weather friends is ultimately meaningless. Yet if they respect you and your strength even if they're weak and worthless as friends/brothers/members of the gang you don't have to worry about them getting one over on you because of the respect they have for you that comes from your strength.

Look at it this way let's say we have two men. Jackson and Tim. Both live in a small town of a couple thousand people or so. Tim has bought into the modern system. He believes that violence is something that should never be tolerated and is never the answer. He believes that the more he does for others the better off he'll be. Nearly the entire community has been impacted by Tim in a positive way. He's opened his house to others, he's work day and night at the battered women's shelter and he's always there every Sunday to give his 10% to the church though of course being Tim he never makes a big deal out of it.

Then we have Jackson. Jackson just got out of prison for a violent altercation. He is ex-military which gives him some respect around the community but other than that is known as a scoundrel. He steals and lives as he pleases. Now let's say something tragic were to befall this town. Let's say the governmental policy of the country where they live has made it to where food is scarce and combined with a nearby war people are starving. A mass of villagers the same villagers that were so helped by Tim and cheated by Jackson band together to scrounge up some food. Tim has stock piled food just for this occasion and offers it to them.

They thank him but soon return for more. Tim gives all he can to them even cutting his own shares to share with the community. Then one day a group of villagers come out to Tim wanting more they say Jackson stole their share of bread. But Tim turns them away and points to Jackson across the street and says "We'll go get it back from him". Jackson sits there watching them through steely eyes knowing on his "ill gotten" bread. The villagers look at Jackson there are three of them there but perhaps they could take him but then they turn to Tim who has another share left. Tim refuses to give it to them. A fight breaks out and Tim is fatally injured in the scuffle. The villagers take all of Tim's bread and leave sprinting past Jackson as he rises from his chair.

You can give someone everything you have but if there is no respect for you they'll simply treat you as a tool to be used and then discarded. Likewise you could take from someone everything but if they have respect for you and your strength then they'll treat you at the very least as an equal but far more likely as a greater. It's human nature, it's not pretty but it's true. The outlaws knows this and has seen this play out and therefore seeks respect first and foremost. If he is hated so be it, it matters little in the grand (and true) scheme.

Real Respect

There is a difference between what one would call true respect and fake respect. One is as we stated above not something that can be negotiated. The villagers who killed Tim couldn't negotiate the respect they had for Jackson though they could and did "negotiate" the "respect" they had for Tim. One was based on strength one was based on he was convenient at the time and social convention. One is based on something that cannot be changed or moved the other is as stable as a leaf blowing in a hurricane. Still one moment than slamming to the ground in the next. Tim found this out the hard way. This is the difference between respect based on strength (real respect) and "respect" based on niceties or morals.

False respect (the one we're "supposed" to give to certain people) means nothing when it comes down to it. It's a mist, an illusion of no real substance and which counts for nothing when the cards are down. Whereas real respect based on strength is a respect that cannot be changed and is always there. This real respect is the only kind of respect that matters. If someone respects you for things other than your strength that respect will fly out the window once they are put under pressure (or even inconvenienced a little) this happens to employees, spouses, and other people time and time again. If you can't destroy someone utterly and completely they're going to have a hard time respecting you and will stab you if it means saving their own skin.

Respect is all, the outlaw knows this. He has lived too close to reality to be foolish enough to rely on the goodness of others, even those within his own gang. He knows what lies behind the plastered smiles and docile nature of the herd.

Someone may like you even "love" you (whatever that word means) yet will turn on you like wolves as soon as it's inconvenient to like or "love" you. Respect is non-negotiable. No one can decide if they want to truly respect you, they simply do at a primal level. Seek out respect based on strength and you'll have a firm base to fight from in this world.

An Outlaw's Loyalty

After describing the outlaw you may be thinking "Sure he may be powerful and masculine, but I don't want to become an amoral sociopath and therefore this isn't for me. But you see the outlaw isn't without morality, kindness, goodness, morality, and all those things that help civilization along when people play nice. Rather he reserves it for those that actually deserve it. So while the average citizen is told to be nice, loving, and loyal to the state and all within the state. The outlaw picks and chooses who he shows kindness and loyalty to. it's isn't something that is freely given it is something that has to be earned and it is not easily earned.

The average citizen is told to be loyal to his enemies and his masters as loyal as he is to his family and friends who (ideally) care about him. How does this make any sense? To be kind and loyal to those who would use and destroy you? The outlaw loyalty is to those that are within his gang, his circle, everyone else is treated as whatever they present themselves to be. If they wish to be an enemy or attempt to enslave to outlaw then they are dealt with. If they are innocent and just happen to be standing by in this world then nothing bad will befall them. As I've said elsewhere the outlaw doesn't seek to enslave others.

It's a pain keeping them in line and the outlaw performs better on his own anyways. He'll fight attempts at one trying to take his own freedom but has no interest in taking the freedom of others simply for taking the freedom of others or for his own ends. Only if one stands in the way of the outlaw does he get dealt with by the outlaw. Those within the outlaw's loyalty are treated with kindness, love, and respect. They are shown softness because they won't attack the outlaw ruthlessly for showing such things as the world as a whole would. They would never use the outlaw and if they tried they would be destroyed for the outlaw has no mercy for his enemies and those that come against him. Even if they do it in a roundabout way.

Loyalty Is Earned

With this being said one doesn't get the outlaw's loyalty simply because he wears the same badge, has the same skin color, or has the same beliefs. Snakes and rats come in all different shapes and forms many similar to the outlaw's own. A outlaw looks at a man's character and judges him based on it. Though he knows he can't be allies with all and doesn't care to be he knows that one of the most important skills he can learn is to be a good judge of character. An outlaw's trust and respect must be earned before his care and kindness are earned. Not only must it be earned but it must be tried and tested as well. He knows anyone can fake something for some time.

Loyalty like respect isn't something that is given out freely. There are no "We're both human so we both deserve respect" that is bullshit. Belonging to the same species does not mean one should respect the other and sets one up for being taken advantage of and destroyed in this world. Wolves tear each other's throats out and man is no better, and may in fact be worse. When you go around with open arms you signal to the entire world that is filled with predators that not only are you weak but that you are also a fool. You are an easy mark, easy prey. You will be taken advantage of until it's better to take you out completely.

Such is the fate of one who gives his loyalty, kindness, and love away freely. However when loyalty must be earned not only does it prevent one from being destroyed so easily but it is also worth much more. No one has respect for the man that "respects all" (if that's even possible) nor does anyone have love for the man who "loves all" for it is then meaningless. While an outlaw may put his life on the line fighting for a brother he'd let the mass of humanity die in a ditch and laugh as he passed. Meanwhile the "man" who "loves all" is doing what? Simply virtue signaling harder and harder to show his love, yet would he lay down his life for every passerby? Even those that'd happily kill him and make use of his family?

Crossed Loyalty

Because the outlaw's loyalty is true and runs so deep it is a deep insult when it is crossed. Cross an outlaw's loyalty and you become something worse than an enemy, you become a traitor. While an enemy can simply be defeated and disposed of a traitor is someone who must be made an example of. Come against someone face to face and toe to toe and when you best your enemy you allow him to die without further ado. However when one comes at your back with a knife then things change. They cannot simply be defeated but must be made as an example of what happens when one crosses your loyalty and kindness.

A former friend turned enemy is always more bitter than one who has been an enemy since the beginning.

A crossed loyalty is one of the greatest of insults as well as a testing of one's strength. Do you allow it to pass or to you make it right? The outlaw always makes it right and makes an example out of those who cross him. Much of these can be prevented by happening by vetting each and every person you give your loyalty to hard and often but even then there are those that simply do not get it and do not care. Those are the ones that an example must be made of. This can happen in business, relationships, war, and every other realm of human endeavors.

When an outlaw's loyalty is crossed he acts like one of the gods of old jealous and all-consuming in their rage when they have been blasphemed. While the outlaw may not cause fireballs to rain from heaven or every first born to die he does what is necessary to ensure that his loyalty is never crossed again and that all know he will not lie down and let others walk on him, especially to those that he has shown his rare kindness and loyalty to. An outlaw's loyalty is hard won and even harder crossed. The outlaw also realizes that the weakness of humanity keeps most from being worthy of loyalty and that humans will turn on one another as soon as they are inconvenienced or pushed. Only a few noble souls are worthy of true loyalty and love.

The Outlaw Plays To Win

Have you ever held back? There are certainly times when it's warranted. For example sparring with a member of your pack, training a student, and a few other times and places when it's acceptable. But once you leave the ring and face someone or something that is not a brother looking to sharpen you and you him or a student looking for your teaching then things change completely. The only thing that counts outside a match is victory or defeat. There are no rules in battle there are only victors and losers. To the victor goes the spoils while death and slavery go to the loser. There is no nobility in defeat outside of the ring. There is no nobility in being defeated in the real world.

The outlaw understands this and always plays to win and always play for keeps. Because that is how the world works. There is a time for training and a time for war. A time to use rules and a time to throw them away completely. The only thing that counts in the real world is winning, there are no second place winners for the most part. When presented with a challenge most have the faulty mindset of using "just enough" of whatever to complete it. They want to use "just enough" brain power, "just enough" effort, and "just enough" force to get what they want. While others use all that they have to take victory. And when these two forces meet one is always blown out of the water because "just enough" is never going to cut it.

"Just enough" ensures defeat when the it really counts. "Just enough" ensures that you'll end up losing more than winning and that's not a way to live a good nor a long life. You must always come ready to go the distance. If you show up to the fight without any fight in you (wanting to do "just enough") then you're not going to make it through plain and simply. Not only must you be willing to go the distance whatever that may be but you must be willing to go the distance and further under harder circumstances than your opponent. That is the direction in which victory lies. No half measures, no lukewarm feelings. A singleness of purpose and an unwavering dedication to your cause and fight.

Staying Sharp

Many live their lives in a sort of haze. They live only half awake unware of what goes on around them. Because of this they make for easy targets and easy pickings. No fool can acquire much for long without it being taken from him by one smarter, quicker, stronger, or just plain better. In order to always be ready to go the distance and fight to win, one must keep himself sharp. An animal that loses his edge is an animal that is slated to die. Not staying sharp is like going into a knife fight with a dull knife. No matter your previous experience or know how you're not going to come out the other side ahead.

Generally life throws us enough to stay sharp on our own. With the challenges that come from every angle, constantly fighting and constantly overcoming whatever is thrown at us keeps us sharp. Yet even with all of that we can keep an ever sharper edge by always maintaining ourselves and training. Maintaining (if not improving) not only our physical body and skills but also our mind and wisdom. It all plays a part in who comes out on top. There is no single one factor that decides everything which is why we must develop them all. Like a fortress that has walls on every side not just a few. A fortress with three walls in the middle of a plain might as well not have any.

Dullness is extinction. When you lose your edge you become prey. You may say "Well yes this is true for the outlaw because of the life that he has lived" but you'd be wrong. It's true for us all. It's just as true for the suburb dad or the corporate drone as it is for the outlaw. We like to think that we live insulated from the way the world works but we don't. We may not face life and death (or we may) but the mechanisms are all still the same. You will still be seen as a target and taken out accordingly. Staying sharp prevents this from happening. Though we all must go eventually.

Show No Mercy, For You Will Be Shown None

Mercy is as they say something that works well as a intratribal ideal but is not for those outside. For those outside you must press every advantage and go for victory at all costs. You must show no mercy for you will be shown none in return and any weakness that you expose will be used against you. Outside the gang's hideout mercy is not used. Even if you were to place arbitrary rules on yourself and they were agreed to as soon as your enemy could they would use them against you. All that happens in this instance is that the honorable are destroyed because of their foolishness of thinking the enemy knows the meaning of honor, something that only exists between groups of men banded together.

Perhaps you will get lucky and face worthy and honorable enemies that share your sense of honor. Even so betting your future on luck is a guaranteed way to end up somewhere you don't want to end up. Not to mention that this world rewards rats, cowards, and cheats more than anything else and if you do have honor and are strong these rats, cowards, and cheats will hate you all the more. They'll hate you for not being the docile sheep they can do as they please with and they'll hate you from standing against the slave masters that pad their pockets so well. Meaning that most of your enemies will come from this class.

A class that cannot be reasoned or talked with but simply destroyed and defeated. They must be met measure by measure and even more. If they use knife use guns, if they use guns use bombs, and so on and so forth. Not playing to win ensures one thing and one thing only. Death, defeat, destruction, or whatever else you want to call it but there is nothing noble or good about it. No matter how you ended up there. And if you're looking for a good name for history when then hell there's nothing better than victory to do that. The victors are always the good guys in the history books no matter how wretched they actually were.

The Duality Of An Outlaw

When it comes to talking about the outlaw it's important to realize that he represents duality if not a paradox of sorts. Here's what I mean by this. I want you to think of the outlaw, what comes to mind? Of course it's going to be different for different people. Some people are going to think of a Hollywood movie portrayal, while another is going to think of a local gang or perhaps their own, while another is going to think about a loner that brings to mind "outlaw" when they think of them. My point is while we may often think of an outlaw as a loner and a fierce individualist the truth of the matter is that outlaws generally reside in gangs. Even a powerful man is not going to last long on his own, when compared to how long he'd last with others around him.

Yet we cannot help but notice an outlaw's love of individuality (by standing out from the masses) as well as a love freedom. An outlaw swears to oath to a loyal and trusted few to declare himself separate from the nothingness that makes up the masses and not having an identity. So the outlaw is both a "rugged individualist" as well as a gang member and leader. He represents what is best about one who wishes to stand on their own two feet with what is best about the practicality of having other men around you on your side. One could learn much from this well balanced duality of the outlaw. One can be an individual without being a fool and one can be part of a group without suffering the same fate.

A lone wolf appeals to the imagination but a strong gang appeals to reality. What the outlaw seeks is a group of "lone wolves" that are simply alone because they live among masses of sheep and yapping sheep dogs. However when these lone wolves become part of a pack they don't suddenly turn into sheep. They stay wolves, but wolves in a pack. That is the outlaw and his gang. They are separate from the masses yet bounded and bonded to one another. One can be both a lone wolf that stands apart from the sheep yet also part of a pack. As a matter of fact that is the ideal that an outlaw strives for. No gang of sheep ever accomplished something and no sheep on his own does anything but feed predators.

The Rugged Individualist

The rugged individualist is an ideal that has caught the mind of many a man and for good reason. The rugged individualist represents what we all want to be. A man who is so strong and powerful that he stands alone, unbowed, against all that this world can throw at him. He walks his own path separate from the bleating sheep. This is an ideal as the lone wolf, rugged individualist, or whatever you would call him doesn't translate quite as well to reality. Sure in an atomized society a strong man (the lone wolf) will always be stronger and more able than any single weak male (sheep). However a lone wolf is pretty much guaranteed to get hunted down by the slave master's sheepdogs who go in groups and will have no mercy on one not in chains.

However as an ideal this has great power. Everyone is the gang should seek to get as strong as they possibly can in order to theoretically stand as a lone wolf as long as they can. They should seek the ideal of the rugged individualist as a lone wolf who could keep the sheep dogs going for days or tear out the throats of many before falling. Of course as I've said and the outlaw believes there is nothing noble in dying or losing. The nobility resides in living and overcoming. Again this is an impossible ideal to strive for. One can never achieve it short of divine intervention, but that's not something I'd be betting on.

But it gives great power. When everyone (or simply you) are striving to be able to face this world alone it brings great strength to you. Facing an impossible task yet fighting with all you have. Not practical but a golden ideal. The rugged individualist represents something deep within man that he wishes to achieve. To have risen above the world and truly conquered it. While one can never do so they can get far, without great ideals there would be no great men throughout the ages. No great conquerors, kings, warriors, or outlaws. It'd be a boring existence without impossible ideals. We'd be a whole lot weaker and a whole lot easier to control.

The Gang Member

Now is where we get practical. One should strive to be the rugged individualist of myth and legend. The hero who slays the dragons single handedly. However that simply isn't going to happen to have a standing in this world you need a gang of brothers, you need a wolf pack. The ideal is a gang of all striving to be the rugged individualist yet watching out and caring for one another at the same time. Many things can brings men together but nothing so much as adversity. Many find themselves in the bond of a gang simply to survive the harsh conditions around them. You cannot go through combat with someone without having a very good chance of that man becoming a brother.

It's not weakness to know that you cannot stand alone in this world, it's wisdom. You should always be looking for those that can aid you and help you and your cause. Imagine that you have a plot of land somewhere deep in the woods and you know that the apocalypse is nigh and you need worthwhile people to survive with. That's how you should treat those that you allow into your life. Remember and outlaw's loyalty is not something that is given out freely but rather is something that must be earned.

You need to be careful who you allow into your circle. Better to be a lone wolf destined for destruction than surrounded by bleating sheep as you slowly contemplate suicide or who scatter at the first sign of distress leaving you out alone. Better to have no friends and allies than to have friends and allies that sabotage you or ditch you when times get tough. At least with no friends and allies you know what's coming and can adjust. It's a whole lot different when you expect others to be there for you and then have to re-strategize in the middle of a fight when they don't show.

Takes What's Best Of Both

Both sides the rugged individualist and the gang member have their bad sides. The rugged individualist is an impossible ideal more likely to get dreamers killed when used improperly as anything else. An the gang member can be nothing more than a sheep that was needed to beef up numbers yet when times get tough will do as all sheep do. You want to take what is good about either side and then combine them into something that is greater than the sum of the parts. The outlaw.

Even if the gang fades the outlaw has strengthened himself enough to stand on his own even if only for a short period of time. The outlaw combines his strength with wisdom allowing to survive above all else. Of course alone he cannot do as much as when he is with like-minded others, he is still a force to be reckoned with. At least as much as any one man can be. It is when outlaws band together that true forces capable of change and self-sustaining come about. Put simply be strong, be wise, be with your brothers, be an outlaw.

An Understanding Of The World Unknown To Most

It has been drilled into our head since childhood that humans are good and that have a good nature within them. We are supposed to believe that deep down everyone is really good, just perhaps misunderstood. The existence of evil and/or an apathetic universe is something that goes over the head of the average person. It just doesn't make sense to them and would blow up all of their fragile beliefs (something they protect no matter how deep they have to bury their head in the sand). The outlaw has been fortunate enough to see humanity for what it really is and the universe for how it truly behaves. Things that most cannot know without spinning into a depression or nihilism or some other weak philosophy.

The outlaw stares at the horror and wretchedness of the world and humanity and smiles. Not because he likes it any more than anyone else but because he knows his comfort (what little can be had) comes from his own strength and not the goodness of others or a universe. Humans will slit each other's throat for a bit of recognition or a sliver of bread (and that's when they're not starving) and the universe does not give a shit whether you live, die, or are tortured for all eternity. No one cares about you any further than it helps them along. This can even be applied to members of the gang.

The outlaw knows that seeing reality and humanity for what it is and they are gives him tremendous power. For he stares at the truth without blinking. And the truth gives on strength. Much more strength than the man or woman burying their heads in the sand. Lying down and rocking back and forth ensures that you'll lose the battle and be an easy target. You must stare at the horror and be strong enough to survive in it. You must keep your eyes wide open and your wits about you. If you want to make it that is. It is a noble and rare soul that shows true loyalty and honor, making a brother worth a damn one of the most valuable things you can ever have.

No One Is Going To Save You

Modern people have been convinced (among other things) that there is someone that is always going to save them. That some government organization or grievance group will always be there to sooth them and give baby what it wants. And maybe that's true for them but it's very doubtful that it'll be true for you.

And even if it was, so what? First off you're making a deal with the devil. Trading your soul, freedom, and balls for some milk from the infected teat of that diseased beast. And second who says it'll last and once they've gotten what they wanted from you they'll throw you into the ditch with everything else that has been sucked of all its value.

Anyone who is reaching a hand out (that isn't a brother) wants something from you, without exception. Everything is a transaction and everything is a deal. Generally a deal in which the other party expects to screw you as much as possible without incurring your wrath (if there's any left). Anything you want in this life must be taken by your own force of will and strength. No one is going to save you, no one cares about you, and no one is going to help you out. Which is fine. We were not born into this world to grow fat and weak like hogs for the slaughter. We were born to be lions, wolves, and eagles whatever animal have you. But one whose life is filled with combat and struggle.

We were made to live not exist, this world is nothing but a passing through. The comfort of this world is largely an illusion and when it's not is poison. Sweet lies will always win out over bitter truth. An outlaw understands this and walks through the world understanding what is around him, the reality of it. Friends are few and often illusionary while enemies, cowards, and degenerates can be found by the bucket full. Throw a coin and you'll hit ten. They'll do nothing but take from you. Use them as you need then discard them, loyalty is reserved for vetted brothers and vetted brothers alone.

"Save" Yourself

If you want something done you do it yourself. If you want something accomplished you go out and accomplish it, plain and simple. The outlaw does not wait for the go ahead or permission from others, especially not authorities (slave masters) who only ever approve of those who will toe the line and be good little slaves (albeit with some more "privileges"). An outlaw sees what he wants he then goes and takes it. The world opens up for those who are strong enough to force their will. Those who rely on themselves and realize that no one is going to do it for them, no one is going to save them, and the cavalry ain't coming, ever. You're here on your own and if you can't cut it you're not going to get saved you're going to get destroyed.

This doesn't mean that one should throw up their hands and cry, bitch, and moan (which solves nothing). It means you've been given the gift of wisdom. No one said it'd be easy and no one said it'd be pleasant but it's needed. Once you see clearly and you mind adjusts to a more realistic view of how the world works you naturally adjust. Sure some can't hack it and become cynics, chronic whiners, and nihilists but the strong, the men, the outlaws simply nod and continue. Fighting the battles they must and ignoring the ones they don't. They world is no longer their concern, they and theirs are the only concern. Let the world crumble it was never a friend (and more likely an enemy) to them anyways.

No one will save you and you don't have to save those outside your group. Harsh? Perhaps. True. Absolutely. Save yourself. Because when it comes down to it that's all you really have and ever will have. Use those outside the group (for they will do far worse to you), trust those within the group (if they merit it), but only completely and absolutely rely on yourself and yourself alone. This the way to survive, this is the way to thrive, this is the way to make sense of a cruel, unforgiving world. You can hack it, as always be strong, be smart, be wise, be an outlaw.

The Outlaw's Unique Path

The outlaw's path is not one that will want (or can be) taken by all. It's a bit ironic never have people been told more that they're "special" and "unique" and yet never has humanity been so without difference. Everyone thinks the same thoughts, believes the same beliefs, and does the same actions. We all fit into a little tiny mold that breaks and destroys us but hey at least they tell us we're special while doing it, and we're dumb enough to believe them. Being an outlaw by its very nature is polarizing you will be disliked by many. Many will envy your freedom, fear your power, and hate that you stand unshackled. Most people don't want to be saved from their misery rather they want others to join them.

A pig wants to wallow in the mud. It's in their nature and anything that gets near them will get dirty with them. To be an outlaw is the separate to be apart from society and mainstream thought as a whole. This is by its nature alienating in a sense. You'll look around you and there will be many that you simply cannot relate to. What does the wolf share in common with a sheep or a lion with a pig? Not much and living among them will do nothing but drive you crazy. This doesn't mean you need to be a hermit just understand that your path will be different. Your path will be harder and more dangerous no doubt. But it will also be one with more freedom and choice.

If you're someone who has to rely on others, who always needs someone's in arms reach then this path is not for you. However if you don't mind get scraped and knocked around as long as you stand on your own two feet in the end, then this may be the path for you. It's outside the mainstream and therefore for those who don't want to be "average" whatever that means anymore. Perhaps in certain societies "average" isn't that bad of a label. The average Spartan is probably a better put together individual than an above average Westerner. Society has a large impact on what is considered "average" yet to get anything above this you can follow the path that is lain out before you. You can move with the crowd but must become separate from it.

The Outlaw's Way

The outlaw's way is to use his own sense to forge a path ahead. Use what experience, wisdom, and guts have taught him about how the world works. To not accept something just because it's "supposed" to be that way. What is "supposed" to be is something that is decided by the slave masters anyways who are no friend of the outlaw (or the slaves, but try telling them that and you'll be met with hostility). The outlaw must walk a path of his own. Like I said above this will at times be lonely and at times you'll have to face things on your own and weather them. There is no flock to run in the middle of hoping for the best. It's you and the elements, you and the world.

This gives you a unique view on how things work. You'll see things that others don't see, experience things that others don't experience, and think thoughts that others don't think (or least pretend like they don't). After all it is the truth that sets one free and if the outlaw is one thing he is free. This isn't to say he isn't human or that he isn't subject to his own biases and forms of group think. But rather that he is for the most part free from whatever spell the herd is currently under. Again for the most part even the slave masters have their own versions of sheep like behavior. We all do, it's minimizing it and not letting others program it that's key.

Being alienated is not always a bad thing. To be sane in a sea of crazy is to be alienated. To be strong is a sea of weakness it to be alienated. These are good types of alienation and one that an outlaw to use to gather those that are like him around him. To find those that are alienated through merit, something that will increase as societies become more corrupt and worship weakness and sickness more and more. Those with healthy minds, bodies, and spirits with vigor in their bones are going to stand out more and more. On one side this will increase the alienation on the other it will allow for gangs to be formed much easier and quicker. It will be easier to see kindred spirits and souls, outlaws that have also been alienated from the sickness around them.

The Two Sets Of Rules

There are two sets of rules those that are governed by reality and cannot be changed. These are the set of rules that the slave masters and the outlaws follow. They are rules where one lives in accordance with reality and all that it entails. Delusions are not tolerated and truth is what matters. Then there are rules created by slave masters for the sheep dogs and sheep so that they may blindly follow and always remain in chains. These rules are based on an understanding of human nature and how to control any herd like animal. They make use of all sorts of social functions, psychology, and brute force when needed to keep the masses in line and all braying and barking on the same note.

The slave masters do not want others to think outside these lines. They want all to follow the rules that they have set out because the rules that they have set out are the ones that benefit them and theirs first and foremost (and often exclusively). Imagine if you were in competition with a business where you made a rule that every transaction the business had it had to give seventy percent of the profit to you. They wouldn't be much of a competition anymore would they? So it is the same with the slave masters, they don't want competition, they want domination. And the sheep dogs and sheep ensure that they get it.

Outlaws are the ones who do not follow what is lain out for them. They are not at home with chains on their backs and in their minds and souls. Outlaws are the only ones that are a threat to the system, though most could honestly care less about the system. So long as they get theirs and theirs are taken care of. The outlaw's way is doing what is best for you. It's about putting yourself first and not backing down from that. There are risks for going the outlaw's way but it is well worth it for those that can stomach it. The outlaw's way is of strength and wisdom as is the way of man. A path few chose but the only path where one can fully become what they were meant to be and perhaps even pass into legend like the outlaws of old.

Snakes & Wolves

I remember reading a story, it might have been when I was a child I don't really know. It was called *The Princess & The Curdie* the main protagonist in the book was giving a blessing, power, or whatever you want to call it where he could tell the nature of a person by shaking their hand. Their hand would be an animal of whatever type of character the person had. So for example a strong noble king when shaking his hand the protagonist would shake with the paw of a lion. Likewise when dealing with someone devious an untrustworthy he'd shake a reptilian hand of some sort, usually the tail of a snake. It's been awhile but that was the gist of it.

The important thing about this is how this relates to reality. Throughout this book I've described people through different animal traits. Traits that are quite accurate. For example sheep dumb as a rock and docile as can be. Wolves independent and fierce. Sheep dogs creatures that exist for their masters will and are at home on a leash. And so on and so forth. While there are no perfect comparisons they do a good job of getting the point across. This reveals a lot about the nature of a person. Looking around you I'm sure you can identify those that fall into the categories just lain out.

I'm sure you recognize sheep, perhaps you've been a sheep or they make up the majority of your family. You've no doubt recognized wolves, hopefully you are one or on your way to becoming one and if you are one this is generally the only group of men you'll ever truly get along with and enjoy. Likewise we all know sheep dogs, happily content at their master's feet licking up the scrapes their master throws them. But there is another group that I haven't described as an animal of any sort and that is the slave masters. I'm sure you know the animal they get, as it's been used throughout time to represent people of this nature. The viper or snake, pick your preference.

The Reptile Society

Let's talk for a moment about reptiles. Putting apart body structure and biology what separates them from animals? Why is it so easy to identify with a talking lion yet a talking lizard or snake doesn't hold the same relation. Sure there are some exceptions but when you look through stories throughout the ages reptiles generally hold the same place. First off reptiles do not have feelings. They cannot love, care, or do anything what we could consider "human". Compare that to a dog that can love, play, and fight for someone he cares about. All very human characteristics. Whereas a snake would eat you alive if it could, even if you'd been its care taker for years (or however long snakes live). They have no "souls".

They live to exist. They live to reproduce and that's it. Sure humans largely fall into this as well but most at least dress this up in trappings of morality or love or something. Reptiles do not have this. They eat, they live, they reproduce. Nothing gets in the way of that. They'll eat and kill young, old, weak, strong, any race, any creed, anything. A crocodile sees you the exact same as he sees a woman, a child, or a squirrel potential food, potential sustenance to continue its existence. Nothing more and nothing less. Again as we've said they have no "soul". Sure we can argue about whether any animal has a "soul" or whatever but that isn't the point here.

The point is snakes are completely amoral and out to further their own existence. They aren't mammalian and they sure as hell aren't human. The slave master's the one's we call snakes are the exact same. They care nothing for the sheep dog's they string along nor for the sheep that they feed on and use as cattle. They hate the wolves because the wolves are the only ones who'd tear their heads off without remorse. The wolves are the only ones who see through their slick exterior to the slime it truly is. So perhaps it's not so crazy to say that we are ruled by reptilians because in a way most of humanity is. Part of being an outlaw is breaking free of the unnatural society of reptiles to the society of mammals. Where freedom, tribe, and honor still mean something. And there is more to life than simply existence.

The Wolves In The Wild

A wolf will never be happy in a reptilian society, no matter what. He'll never be happy living for something that cares nothing for him. There is no benefit (and in fact much detriment) for the snakes to keep reproducing and going. Unlike the sheep dogs who live to keep the sheep in line for food for the snakes and the sheep who live for comfort even if it's in exchange for being food for the snakes the wolf needs to live for himself and his wolf pack. Wolf packs are something else that the snakes (often using the sheep dogs) make sure don't have a chance to gather together and become a threat to the dominance of the snakes.

Wolf packs are strong and resilient. Strike down the alpha of a wolf pack and another will grow to take his place and perhaps be out for revenge. Whereas snakes don't even trust each other, cut off one's head and the rest will devour whatever's left within moments. I don't know if this is the exact behavior of these animals but that's not the point here. The snakes and the wolves cannot exist together within the same sphere. They are at odds with one another by the very nature of what they are. They are two parts of creation that cannot both habitat the same area and both fight for supremacy.

Naturally the wolf could gut the snake so the snake had to resort to more devious methods for dominance. One of which was recruiting the sheep and sheep dogs to do their bidding and increase their power. However what a snake wants most if dominance and what a wolf wants most is freedom. But that's enough of that. Understand the nature of those that want to control and what their end goal is. The eradication of wolves (their only true threat). Conversion to sheep or more likely well-heeled sheep dog would be better but of them all the wolf is the hardest to convert to anything else. Be free, be a wolf.

Gaining Freedom In An Unfree World

Gaining freedom in an unfree world is something that deep down every man desires for himself and those he cares about. After all freedom is directly tied to one's sense of masculinity and manhood. It's hard if not impossible for a slave to feel like a man. We've discussed what separates the outlaw from the average citizen. What separates the wolf from the sheep and the rest of society. Following the path of the outlaw is a step towards freedom, it's a step towards reclaiming your mind and therefore your life. There are rich men that are slaves likewise free men that have less to their name than you do. Of course there are poor men who are slaves and rich men who live lives of freedom.

Money alone will not get you what you want, though it plays a part. Freedom is something much deeper than that. Simply breaking free of your cubicle isn't always enough especially if you end up in a plantation of another kind. Switching from being a slave in one industry to another doesn't do you any good. Many who wanting to get out of the cubicle farm break free and start their own business but end up an even bigger slave to that business. Of course there are also many who have broken free, started their own business and now are living the life that they've always wanted and that fits much better with their mind, body, and soul (something a cubicle will never do for the wolf).

Freedom isn't a simply topic. As we've stated some rich are free, some poor, some working in a place where another would rather die, and vice versa. Freedom is a multi-faceted ideal that stems from many different places. Also I should note I'm not talking about "freedom" in the political sense whatever the hell that means anymore. I'm talking about freedom to be one's own man, or at least as much is possible in this world. Freedom requires many things to be acquired but they have far less to do with what is on the outside for example x amount of income, certain status, or achieving a certain set goal and rather has much more to do with what is on the inside.

Freedom Starts In The Mind

A free man is first and foremost free in his mind. I'll explain what this means. Freedom starts in the mind, meaning that regardless of the external things that one has a big bank account, a high paying job, a gorgeous wife, a loving family, a house in a third world country where they can live as kings, or whatever is commonly considered ideal yet they remain a slave in their mind will never experience freedom. A free mind is the healthy ground from which the tree of freedom can spring. Perhaps that sounded a little cheesy but you get the point. Without a free (meaning healthy) mind achieving freedom is something that will elude you.

Most would recommend going about this by becoming detached from the world in some sort of Buddhist fashion but as any man knows that's a great way to get killed. You must not become detached from the world but rather engage it and enforce your will upon it, a mindset that must be embraced to gain freedom. Freedom doesn't come from nothingness and numbness it comes from strength and understanding. We've talked about breaking free of the slave morality of working day and night and putting the needs of your masters above all else. Gaining freedom starts with putting yourself first and foremost and working for yourself first and foremost.

From that core is where everything else stems. Putting yourself first and then taking a realistic view of the world. People are not your friends, they are not inherently good, and they are not wise in any way. This doesn't mean you hate them it simply means you see them for who and what they are. Your loyalty, care, kindness, and everything else is reserved for vetted people within your gang, tribe, family, or whatever you want to call it. It isn't something given out freely to any passerby because they're part of the "brotherhood of humanity" or some other delusional term designed to defang and neuter you. This world never stopped being kill or be killed, it always has been and always will be in some form.

Freedom In The World

The freeing of your mind is step one and from that other growth can take place and naturally things follow from freeing your mind. For example once you first start living for yourself and realize that essentially everyone out there is out for theirs as well it allows you to take action to better yourself and your situation. You don't work tirelessly for those that hate you or care less about you. You work tirelessly to gain strength and wisdom for yourself so that you can fight your way through this world more victorious than not. Freedom comes from conquering and strength. Sort of like the only way to truly have peace is through superior firepower, everything else is a false peace. It'll be peace until it's not advantageous for the stronger side in which case the weaker side will be quickly crushed.

Freedom stems from a free mind which leads to the attainment of strength and wisdom for oneself. Right thinking leads to right action which leads to right results. Sort of like a strong house can only be built upon a strong foundation. I'm sure we've all heard the story of the man who built his house upon the sand as opposed to the one who built his house upon the rock. The one in the sand didn't last very long. Neither will freedom without the proper mindset, actions, and skills. No matter if you start a company that is profitable, move out to the wilderness with nothing but a gun and some tools, or whatever your version of freedom implies. Without the right mindset and the right actions and skills that proceed from that mindset your freedom will be short lived.

You have to fix the problem at the root and the root is the mind. This book should have more than opened your eyes to mindsets that have been instilled in you that are not for your benefit and whose sole purpose is to keep you in chains. Whether it's the American dream (whatever that means), being a "good" person (according to the slave masters), loving everyone equally, or any other perverted ideology drilled into your head to make you love your chains. Freedom starts in the mind and proceeds from a correct mindset. The outlaw's mindset if you have any questions about what that is then reread the book. But it all starts with this, the outlaw looks out for himself first and foremost. Something you'd be wise to follow.

About The Author

Enjoyed the content? Then could you do me a favor? Leave a review on Amazon or tell a friend about the ways that the book has helped you. I love reading how my books have positively affected the lives of my readers. I read each and every review, they mean a lot to me. If you want to learn more I run a blog at charlessledge.com where you can find more content to further your masculine devclopment to new heights. If you found value in the book drop by and join the community. Looking forward to hearing from you.

-Charles Sledge

Printed in Great Britain
by Amazon

The Assertiveness Book for Women

A Step-by-Step Guide to a Brave & Courageous New You!

Penny Goldman

© **Copyright 2021 - All rights reserved.**

The content contained within this book may not be reproduced, duplicated, or transmitted without direct written permission from the author or the publisher.

Under no circumstances will any blame or legal responsibility be held against the publisher, or author, for any damages, reparation, or monetary loss due to the information contained within this book, either directly or indirectly.

Legal Notice:

This book is copyright protected. It is only for personal use. You cannot amend, distribute, sell, use, quote, or paraphrase any part, or the content within this book, without the consent of the author or publisher.

Disclaimer Notice:

Please note the information contained within this document is for educational and entertainment purposes only. All effort has been executed to present accurate, up to date, reliable, complete information. No warranties of any kind are declared or implied. Readers acknowledge that the author is not engaged in the rendering of legal, financial, medical or professional advice. The content within this book has been derived from various sources. Please consult a licensed professional before attempting any techniques outlined in this book.

By reading this document, the reader agrees that under no circumstances is the author responsible for any losses, direct or indirect, that are incurred as a result of the use of the information contained within this document, including, but not limited to, errors, omissions, or inaccuracies.

Table of Contents

DEDICATION 1

INTRODUCTION 3

CHAPTER 1: WHAT IS ASSERTIVENESS? 7
    WHAT HAPPENS IF WE'RE NOT ASSERTIVE? 9
    BENEFITS OF ASSERTIVE BEHAVIOR 12
    WHAT SHOULD WOMEN ASK FOR? 13
        What's the Worst That Could Happen? 14
    4 STEPS TO DETERMINING THE CHANGES YOU SHOULD MAKE 17
        Step One: Invest in a Journal 17
        Step Two: Find Your Personalized Version of Assertive 17
        Step Three: An Honest List 18
        Step Four: Make Your Goals SMART 18
    HOW DO I KNOW WHEN I GET THERE? 20

CHAPTER 2: IT ALL STARTS WITH BELIEVING IN YOURSELF 23
    STEP 1: LET'S GET TO KNOW YOU A LITTLE BETTER 24
        Question 1: Can I Quote You? 25
        Question 2: Let's Talk About Values 26
        Question 3: Do You Believe in Limits? 26
        Question 4: What Are Your Strengths? 28
        Question 5: Do You Remember When? 29
    STEP 2: SHOW YOURSELF LOVE AND CARE 30
        Surround Yourself With Positivity 30
        Be Kind to Yourself 31
    STEP THREE: LEARN TO TAKE RISKS 32
        Make Calculated Risks 33
        Step Out of Your Comfort Zone 33
        Make a Suggestion 34

CHAPTER 3: TRANSFORM YOUR COMMUNICATION SKILLS 35
    HOW TO ADAPT YOUR VOCABULARY 37
        Say "I..." 38

- WORDS ASSERTIVE WOMEN DON'T USE 40
- HOW TO SAY "NO" 44
  - "No" With a Reason 44
  - The Broken Record Method 45
  - The Vigorous "No" 48
- HOW TO ACCEPT COMPLIMENTS FOR WHAT THEY ARE 48
  - Why You Should Accept Compliments 49
  - How You Should Accept Compliments 50
- SHOULD YOU APOLOGIZE? 51
  - How Should You Stop Saying Sorry? 52
  - If You're Running Late 52
  - If You're About to Interrupt Someone 52
  - If You're About to Complain 52
  - In Emails 53
  - When You're About to Ask or Answer a Question 53
  - When You Can't Go to Work or Need Time Off 54
  - When You Need Help 54
  - When You Need to Express Yourself or How You're Feeling 55

CHAPTER 4: SETTING AND KEEPING HEALTHY BOUNDARIES 57

- WHY DO YOU NEED BOUNDARIES? 58
- STEP ONE: IDENTIFY AND NAME YOUR BOUNDARIES 60
- STEP TWO: COMMUNICATE YOUR BOUNDARIES 61
- STEP THREE: WHEN YOUR BOUNDARIES ARE CHALLENGED 62
- STEP FOUR: PRACTICE SELF-CARE AND MAKE TIME FOR YOU! 66
  - Have a Schedule and Stick to It 67
  - Limit Phone Interactions 68
  - Working Overtime 68
  - Don't Always Be Reachable 69
  - In Your Relationships 70
  - Always Make Suggestions 71
  - Give a Strategic Response…Always! 71

CHAPTER 5: REGULATE EMOTIONS AND BODY LANGUAGE 73

- LET'S TALK ABOUT YOUR FEELINGS 75
  - Identify Your Emotions 75
  - The Power of Emotional Intelligence 77
- LET'S TALK ABOUT BODY LANGUAGE 81
  - Become Visible 81
  - Work on Your Presentation 82
  - Capitalize on Vocal Tone and Rhythm 83

Capitalize on Your Facial Expression and Posture 86
An Activity for Your Body Language: Put on a Killer Act! 86
How to Use Body Language for Assertiveness in Challenging Situations
.... 88
Body Language in Difficult Conversations 88
Body Language for Interviews and Negotiations 90

CHAPTER 6: LET'S RESOLVE CONFLICT AND COMMUNICATE INSTEAD 93

In Comes Confrontation! 95
It All Starts With a Problem 95
How to Handle a Confrontation 97
How to Make Requests and Communicate Effectively During the Confrontation 98

CONCLUSION 107

REFERENCES 111

Dedication

To Ceri: May your sun always shine brightly

Introduction

As a woman, when you stand up for yourself, make bold statements such as "no," or show unanticipated confident behavior, you can often be labeled as aggressive, difficult, or angry by those around you.

Research shows that as opposed to men, women of all ages struggle with being assertive whether it is in the workplace environment, in their relationships, or in society.

You know you're a skilled employee who is overworked and underpaid but you simply cannot walk into your manager's office and raise these points. You often find yourself unhappy in your relationships because if people don't force you to agree to certain decisions, they simply make them for you! For as long as you remember, you've always known just what to say or do but have been scared to blurt the words out or make the changes out of fear of seeming belligerent, or perhaps you worry about hurting people's feelings. This type of fear doesn't only exist in your mind, but you also carry it in the way you speak, the deep breaths you take before you finally oblige to something you are not comfortable with, and the unbearable exhaustion you feel simply because the burden is too much for you to carry.

There is no denying that being in these types of situations leaves you feeling emotionally drained, deeply unhappy, and frustrated. To be honest, these are not catch 22 situations because you are simply putting other people first at your expense. You spend months and months thinking about how to change the situation. You try to formulate a better way of approaching it, and every single time, you are brought to the same conclusion: You need to be more assertive because the ball is in your court—and your court only.

The interesting part is that research also reveals that women are less assertive than men, not because they aren't courageous, but simply because they struggle with ways of exercising assertiveness.

Understanding the role assertiveness plays means that one day you can walk into your manager's office and find yourself discussing your pay raise. You can finally talk to your roommate about their bad habit of smoking in your house, or even say "no" the next time you are pushed to engage in an activity you are not interested in.

Imagine being finally able to let it all out! At long last, you'll be able to fully live and speak your truth because you will be putting yourself first. Not only will you stop being a "yes woman," but you will also earn the respect you've been longing for. In any given situation, you will walk away knowing that both parties are deeply satisfied and that you have improved your communication skills. The exhaustion you're feeling, the mental weariness hanging over you, and the constant deep breaths will be released once and for all. All of this is possible if you simply choose assertiveness in your life!

As you approach every chapter in this book, you need to ask yourself why you are reading this book and what you're trying to achieve. Are you trying to learn more ways of saying no? Do you want to learn how to set boundaries or are you on a quest to learn better ways of handling conflict? It is crucial to identify what led you to this book. By identifying your 'why,' you will be setting yourself up for success because every time you try to give up, your 'why' will remind you why you started in the first place. You know you are tired of the way you've been living and approaching these difficult situations, so may your 'why' drive you until the last page.

Think about what you'll achieve by the time you finish this book. While your 'why' might be an emotional motive driving you to the last page, your achievement is a physical one to be executed even when the book is closed.

In this book, you'll learn how to master the skill of assertiveness so you'll never have to worry about compromising what you really want, hurting other people's feelings every time you say no, or seeming too aggressive or difficult whenever you speak your mind. By following the steps guidelines in this book, you'll work toward never worrying about these issues again!

Are you ready to live your life as the assertive woman you've always been destined to be?

Keep reading!

Chapter 1:

What Is Assertiveness?

Nobody can make you feel inferior without your consent. –Eleanor Roosevelt

Psychologists say that being assertive means "being able to stand up for your own rights, communicating your wants, needs, positions, and boundaries in a calm and clear manner while respecting other people's thoughts and wishes" (Brand Minds, 2019, para. 5).

We often struggle with being assertive because we are driven by a deep fear of not being able to please others. Instead of putting our needs first, we fall into the habit of prioritizing another person's needs and their circumstances and neglect how we might be feeling at that time or how their actions (and words) might be making us feel.

We shouldn't be blaming ourselves for this because as women, we have been preconditioned to believe that we are supposed to be understanding of every person's situation and their feelings. From the beginning of time, femininity has often been associated with softness and the ability to be submissive. Think about it, when you are faced with a difficult situation that requires you to be assertive, you will often find yourself struggling between being too nice, which is going to make you look weak and vulnerable, or being courageous enough to stand your ground, which might make you seem aggressive and difficult. Which way do you often end up approaching these situations? I bet it's more often than not in the nicest way possible!

It becomes clear that a woman's lack of courage and boldness stems from the fear of not acting according to the preconceived gender stereotype that has been embedded in our feminine DNA. We believe that we'll be punished if we dare step out of the little corners set for us. We don't want to speak out about the things people do that make us uncomfortable because we fear jeopardizing our relationships, and the simple thought of saying "no" to someone or something stirs up our anxieties. Most of the time, we don't even know how we're going to react if someone starts challenging us so we avoid conflict at all costs. Some of us even fear speaking out to avoid seeming arrogant or overselling ourselves.

The minute this fear creeps into your mind, you immediately find yourself downplaying the whole situation and then settling for what is considered acceptable behavior for a woman. You internally calm yourself down and begin to make excuses that show you in a negative light. For example, you want to speak to your boss about working fewer hours because you feel exhausted, or you don't like it when your partner suddenly talks down to you whenever you're in a public setting. These issues eat you up and often leave you feeling frustrated. Every day, you rehearse the little speech that you intend to deliver to your boss or your partner. You finally tell yourself you're ready to let it all out until that fear comes crashing down into your whole being. You pause and begin to rethink the whole situation. *Why am I being so difficult? My department is understaffed, and besides, these are the kind of things that are going to make me stand out and earn a promotion. Why am I so mad at my partner for this? Of course, he was just joking! I know the type of person he is.*

This means that no matter how pressing a matter is to you, the fear is going to prevent you from dealing with it because you have given it the power to do so. However, if you consider the definition provided above, you will realize that there is nothing to fear when you're trying to be assertive because as long as it's done in a clear and respectful manner, you'll get your points across.

After looking at some of the side-effects of not being assertive, the benefits of finding our assertiveness, and discussing what women deserve, you will find four clear steps on how to identify changes you should make so you can begin your path toward becoming your ultimate assertive self.

What Happens if We're Not Assertive?

In 2012, a 15-year-old schoolgirl named Malala Yousafzai was shot in the head for speaking up about the rights of girls to be educated in her country, Pakistan. While she fought for her life in hospital, activists, politicians, and the general public from all over the world reacted with an intense shock. Why would you want to deny a young girl her rights to basic education? Is she so powerful that the only way you can silence her is with a bullet? And finally, many people thought she would have avoided all of this by simply keeping quiet and complying with the rules set out by her government.

While it's true that the incident could've been avoided if she had remained compliant like most of the other girls, Malala was driven by a deep passion to speak and live her truth. Most women are trying so hard to live like this; they simply don't know how to tackle the obstacles that are thrown their way.

For a minute, imagine what would've happened if Malala did not make this bold move of speaking out about this unfair injustice. The world may have never paid so much attention to this issue or even taken initiative to help the girls, Malala would've never been the youngest person to ever win a Nobel Peace Prize—and most critically—she would still be living an oppressed life.

Not that you should necessarily aspire to win a Nobel prize or single-handedly change the world, but you should never underestimate the power of living your truth (or the impact of not living it)! Every time you bolt out of a situation that requires you to be assertive, you will find yourself losing more confidence in yourself as you doubt your self-worth and self-esteem. This will leave you wondering whether you truly deserve to get more out of a situation or be treated better.

Lack of courage also leaves you feeling frustrated because you may find yourself hanging in a win-lose situation. This happens when the other party walks away having gained while you sacrificed something that actually matters to you. For example, let's say you're trying to negotiate working hours with your manager. You know you can no longer spend so much time being at the office. You're physically tired, not paid enough for what you're doing, and you're suffering from missing out on time with your loved ones. If you lack the courage to get these points across to your manager, by the end of the meeting, you end up in what is called a win-lose situation. Your manager walks away having gained an employee who will put in more hours and work, which is good news for the company—increased productivity means more money made! You, on the other hand, will continue to drain your body, spend less time with your family, and gain no financial benefit. No one wants to be in these kinds of situations, so it's crucial to take control of them with assertiveness and courage.

As you continue to suppress your feelings you will begin to have a buildup of negativity around your life. You will walk and talk like a frustrated person because that is how you're really going to be. The worst part about this is that frustrated people end up becoming angry people; they just don't know how to react to being undervalued and ignored. Think about it, are you really going to act like a happy person when you are busy working 45 hours a week for absolutely nothing? Not only are you going to be angry but you're also going to resent the people who make you endure the work that leads to those feelings.

One of the most discouraging things about win-lose situations is that the relationship between the two parties is not a candid one. Remember that if you tend to be unable to express how you truly feel in your relationship, the other party can't know for certain where they actually stand with you. Not only is this unfair on them, but it is something that is also going to strain you. You end up being unhappy, cheated out of situations, and holding on to unsatisfactory relationships. That is not fair to you or the person you are in a relationship with.

However, the most important thing to note here is that whenever we pass on the opportunity to voice our concerns or gain enough courage to make the necessary changes in our situations and relationships, we subtly tell people that we are okay with being undervalued or being taken advantage of. We allow them to use this information against us, they will continue to treat us the way we allow them to because even if we don't want them to do that, we are not making it clear to them. In other words, once we show people that we are okay with being treated unfairly, they will continue with this cycle because how else would they know any differently?

So, in the end, it is apparent that the power of making changes in our lives and relationships lies in our hands. Are you ready to challenge yourself?

Benefits of Assertive Behavior

Once you have mastered the skill of being assertive, you will be able to communicate your feelings and desires more clearly and efficiently. This means that even if you do not give another person what they want, they will still walk away from the conversation knowing that you were not malicious or spiteful by standing your ground. They will also make an effort to meet your expectations because you have effectively communicated how important your needs are to you. Everyone longs to be heard and understood, and that is the first thing you're going to achieve.

You will feel so much better about yourself knowing that you've been heard, understood, and are going to have your expectations met.

Once your expectations are met, you will no longer deal with win-lose situations. This is because every time you express yourself or negotiate an outcome of a situation, you'll step out of that conversation having gained something. There will be no more settling, resistance, or lack of self-esteem because the people you will be negotiating with have learned to value and treat you better.

As people begin treating you the way you deserve to be treated, you will find yourself making and maintaining healthy relationships because both parties are honest with each other.

There will be no more unhappiness, anger, or resentment toward these people because both sides will be able to actively compromise to make the relationships work.

Finally, what could be better than getting exactly what you want or need? Do you want fewer working hours? Done! Do you need your partner to start speaking to you more in your love language? You got it! Have you finally asked your roommate to stop smoking inside the house when you're not around? Yes, that can also come true! From here on, you can live the life you've always wanted and you'll do it fearlessly and unapologetically. Believe me, there is no disadvantage to learning to stand up for yourself. Assertiveness is a skill that can unlock your potential to live the life you've always wanted for yourself!

What Should Women Ask For?

In this day and age, women all over the world are desperate for so many things. Some struggle to find partners who treat and respect them as equals, with constant battles over childcare and domestic chores continually raging. Others are pressured into marriages and have children before they are ready. Many women are struggling with equality at work, strapped with the added challenge of piercing the "glass ceiling." Whatever stage we're at, we all want more equality and for our voices to be heard. Developing assertiveness is a skill that will give you that and so much more.

Let's be honest, women also find themselves struggling to stand up for themselves in their relationships with family members. Can you think of a time you avoided a family gathering simply because you're dreading being judged and questioned about the choices you've made in your life? Although you'll be physically present throughout the gathering and might help prepare a salad or two, in your mind, you've already packed your bags and are driving as fast and as far away as you can from your family.

Now, moving to the workplace environment, did you know that in the US, women earn 84% less than their male counterparts (Barroso & Brown, 2021)? This means that it does not matter how qualified you are, which position you hold at work, and how great you are at what you do, if you are a woman, chances are, you're just not going to be paid what you deserve!

These are sad realities that we battle with, but if we're going to be assertive, then we must ask one important question: What should women be asking for. In fact, I should make it a little more personal and ask what should *you* be asking for?

More often than not, we already have the answers to this question, but we struggle verbalizing them because of the fear that we always must accommodate. It makes us doubt our answers and ultimately forces us to settle for things that we know we shouldn't even entertain. One of the only ways that you can conquer this is by being true to yourself when answering this critical question.

What's the Worst That Could Happen?

One of the reasons why we struggle with assertiveness is because we fear disappointing people or hurting their feelings. However, it's important to note that you are not responsible for other people's feelings. Of course, you should always respectably approach them, but you can't neglect your feelings to please the next person. Remember you've been living most of your life in this way, and you're reading this book to eliminate any negative feelings these behaviors have caused.

American writer, producer, and actress, Issa Rae once spoke out about her fear of being assertive. She started her entertainment career by creating a comedic web series on YouTube. The series garnered so much success that Rae had to transition from making digital content to collaborating with big Hollywood shots such as prolific TV writer Shonda Rhimes. Rae recalled a time where she would meet up with executives and they would all agree on certain decisions about her productions that she wasn't particularly excited about. "As a showrunner, being in the industry, just as a woman, once you're labeled like difficult, your career is kinda over, cuz then it's like everybody's saying, 'Oh she's hard to work with, beware,' and then you don't get many chances to fail" (2018, para. 3). Later, she had a conversation with her mentor Shonda Rhimes. Rae reveals that Rhimes told her that there was a time in her life when she took the bold step of speaking up, even though she did not know at that time that she could get fired! Despite Rhimes admission, that's exactly what gave her courage and allowed her to build the successful career she has today. Now, Rae operates with the mentality of having the courage to speak up because you simply don't know what might happen.

You're probably thinking *but that's exactly why I avoid being assertive. I fear not knowing what might happen to me, my job, or relationships if I stand my ground.* Yet, despite these worries, you need to consider this: What really is the worst that could happen?

In 2016, The European Journal of Work and Organizational Psychology published results of a study that revealed that "assertive women were compensated better than their less assertive colleagues" (Hagi, para. 2). This means that chances are it won't hurt your pocket book to try showing some assertiveness, even if you fear the outcomes.

The first step of demonstrating assertiveness is by effectively communicating your true intentions and what you need. Whether you will get your requests fulfilled or not, as long as you can conquer getting your points across you can count this as an achievement. Remember that people might be thrown off by your boldness the first time you stand up for yourself, and even though they might not respond or react in the way you anticipate, they will still go and think about what you said and will probably come back with a solution that might be at least somewhat beneficial for you. There is no need to get discouraged at this point as you can use this as an opportunity to build yourself up for the next situation that might demand assertiveness.

Even if you continue to not get what you desire, you have an opportunity for growth. You now have a chance to rethink the situation or your relationships. Should you build the courage to leave a relationship that appears to be one-sided? Should you look for a better job in a company that will respect you as an employee? Assertiveness is not only about speaking up for yourself, but it is also about being courageous enough to leave a table that no longer serves you.

The worst that can happen to you by not practicing assertiveness is that you will continue to make unreasonable compromises and end up living an unhappy life. Because you have already lived through these dreadful circumstances, doesn't it make sense to try out something different that could potentially bring you positive results?

4 Steps to Determining the Changes You Should Make

Step One: Invest in a Journal

Did you know you are 42% more likely to succeed if you write your goals down? (Forleo, 2019). Being able to develop the habit of thinking deeply about your feelings and goals is the first step that is going to give you the courage to go out there and make them a reality.

If you prefer putting pen to paper, it can be a physical one you're able to write in; if you're more partial to technology, there are many note-taking programs for your phone or laptop. If neither of these options suits you, then you can invest in an app that will allow you to speak and record your thoughts, intentions, progress, and wins.

Step Two: Find Your Personalized Version of Assertive

Once you have a journal, you are going to establish what it means for you to be assertive. Are you more focused on drawing boundaries than communicating your needs? Do you wish you could speak more about your desires in a calm manner without stepping on anyone's toes? Or are you desperately trying to embody the ultimate definition of what this virtuous trait is by ticking all the boxes?

There is nothing wrong with any of these tendencies. Knowing what assertiveness means to you is what is going to make you succeed in your journey because you will be able to identify the steps you need to get there. You'll also be tracking your progress in your journal as you attempt to make changes in your life. There is no need to think long and hard about this because there is no right or wrong answer! Grab your journal and start writing about your own personalized view of the most assertive you.

Step Three: An Honest List

Now that you have discovered your own personal image of assertiveness, you can start your list. Make a list of things you have always wanted to ask for. These could be rights you've always wanted to advocate for, wants and needs that you believe are being neglected, changes you want to make in your career or relationships, and boundaries you'd like to draw. Don't overthink what could go wrong or how hard it's going to be to achieve these things. This exercise simply requires you to be deeply honest with yourself about the changes you'd like to see in your life. Don't be modest; you deserve more than you've been given!

Step Four: Make Your Goals SMART

Finally, break down your list by ensuring that you have goals you can visualize and achieve. The best way to do this is to craft them in the SMART goal design. This means they are specific, measurable, achievable, realistic, and timely.

For example, let's say you have three things on your list:
1. You want to talk to your partner about spending more (or less) time together.

2. You want to learn how to communicate your needs clearly and respectfully.
3. You believe you deserve to earn a little more than you're making now.

Now, let's break them down and make them SMART goals. For the purpose of this exercise, we'll use all of the above to fit them into the SMART goal criteria. However, you should explore all of them individually.

Specific: Is your goal clear and well defined?

Looking at the first item on the list, do you want your partner to consider giving you more time to rest by only going out with you on a date night once a month? Or do you feel like they always make abrupt plans, which often force you to neglect any prior plans you might've made with your family or friends?

Measurable: How are you going to check that you're making progress?

Let's continue using the first item as an example. Do you want to use the first three days to formulate a clear and concise message for your partner in your journal, and then take another day to practice how you're going to say it before finally talking on the fifth day? Moving from one step to the next is progress. As long as you can achieve the results in the end.

Achievable: Remember to always set yourself up for success. Are you sure you're eligible for a pay raise during your first year of working in your company? Always remember to think about the rules and regulations that have been put in place.

Realistic: Is this goal relevant to you right now and is it within reasonable reach?

Maybe you deserve a pay raise, but is the amount you have in mind the standard pay rate for the type of job you have? Or do you want to spend more time with your partner but it's nearly impossible because of the type of schedule they have? Put these into consideration but don't allow them to change your mind.

Timely: Establish a sense of urgency around your goal by creating a timeline that is going to help you succeed.

Have a start and end date and make sure you stick to them! Another way of setting yourself up for success is by ensuring that all of your goals have different start and end dates so that you don't end up being overwhelmed by having to tackle too many issues at once.

Congratulations on your progress, you are on your way to making necessary changes in your life!

How Do I Know When I Get There?

Most women give up because they believe that having the courage and being able to stand up for themselves is something that happens overnight. This is the kind of mentality you should get rid of because it is going to hinder you from achieving success.

Using the timeline you formulated in the previous step, you should be able to track your progress. Don't get discouraged if you fall behind by a day or two; remember that you are trying to master a complex skill. As long as you pick yourself up and continue being focused, you are definitely going to get there. For example, you might succeed at voicing out your concerns over an issue you have in your relationship, but maybe you might unexpectedly find yourself raising your voice, saying a few inappropriate and mean comments, or even walking out before concluding the conversation. That's completely okay, at least you've learned that even though you succeeded at getting a point across, you now have to figure out how to keep calm and respectful during a discussion.

In most cases, we know we are making progress by the way people respond to our requests. Getting some form of resistance from them doesn't necessarily mean you are being unreasonable; it simply means they don't know how to react because they've never experienced you like that. In these situations, it's okay to give them space and allow them to digest what you've presented to them. During this stage, you will experience some form of exhilaration because you have finally expressed yourself. Later on, that dreadful fear will creep in and have you thinking that you might've been unfair and selfish by speaking out, but as long as you have identified that fear, then you can manage it by reminding yourself why speaking out or setting boundaries is important for you.

You will know you have "gotten there" once you start feeling better about yourself. In any situation, you will put yourself first by constantly thinking about your self worth and feelings. You will know you are assertive when the thought of having a discussion or expressing yourself does not make you nervous or feel bad about yourself. If there's still any doubt, you can revisit the steps to be sure that you are getting what you want, saying "no" without hesitation, and remaining calm and respectful even in difficult discussions.

It will not happen overnight, but if you are well on your way if you:

- Get a journal

- Establish what it means to be assertive
- Make a list of your wants
- Break down your list using SMART goals.

By following these steps, you have identified the changes, unique to you and your goals. From here you are one step closer to developing your most assertive self.

Chapter 2:

It All Starts With Believing in Yourself

If you haven't confidence in self, you are twice defeated in the race of life. With confidence, you have won even before you have started. –Marcus Garvey

How do you feel about yourself? Are you kind enough to yourself to accept that you're a flawed human being who is also amazing in her own special way?

There is no doubt that confidence and assertiveness are interconnected. When you think about it, you need some level of boldness to be able to speak up for yourself or draw boundaries with people who have become too comfortable with overstepping into your space; however, this does not mean that if you're not confident you're going to fail at being assertive.

To be more assertive, you need to work at achieving a better understanding of yourself. This means that you'll have to embrace who you are as a person, your life purpose, and what you believe in. At first, it will seem like a difficult task to manage, but as you continue to actively learn to form a better relationship with yourself, you will begin to believe in yourself and your ability to be assertive.

This chapter will show you three easy steps to help you truly believe in yourself. The steps will break down how to:

1. Get to know yourself
2. Show yourself love
3. Take risks

Step 1: Let's Get to Know You a Little Better

To have a deeper understanding of who you are, you'll have to answer a few questions that are going to uncover your true essence and help kick off psychological activities that will help you achieve all of the things you wrote down in the first chapter. These questions are designed to help you value yourself more, remind you of who you really are, and teach you to trust yourself as you embark on this meaningful journey.

Research shows that apart from a child's genetic makeup, where and how they were raised affects how they behave as adults. This does not mean that your parents are to blame for your lack of assertiveness, but it certainly suggests that your childhood had a lot of influence on how you feel about yourself now. If you grew up being constantly told or treated like you're stupid, then it's probably difficult for you to believe in your mental capabilities as an adult. This also applies to being compared to your peers or being treated differently in an environment simply because you did not live up to the expected standards of that territory.

These sorts of treatments and statements, which are called limiting beliefs, are later so strongly embedded in your mind that you actually begin to believe them. In essence, limiting beliefs are negative and often untrue opinions that a person believes to be the absolute truth. They are very dangerous thoughts to live by because they prevent you from growing or reaching your full potential in life.

In this chapter, not only are we going to identify these false statements that you have been living by in your life, but we are also going to start exploring the positive things that you have been overlooking that have the potential to set you up for success.

Using your journal, explore the questions below as truthfully and extensively as you can. Remember, there is no right or wrong answer, and most importantly, no one knows you better than yourself!

Question 1: Can I Quote You?

What is a favorite quote you live by? Make sure your quote is positive, energizing, and inspirational.

Once you have written it down, take it a step further by including it in your personal space. You could either write it on A4-sized paper and put it on your wall or set it as your wallpaper on your phone. Either way, you should be able to read it out loud to yourself every time you see it, preferably more than twice a day.

Question 2: Let's Talk About Values

Values are basic and unique beliefs that you live by. They express the person you aspire to be and guide you to make important decisions about all aspects of your life. How you treat people, approach difficult situations, and interact with the world is all dependent on these elemental values.

Write down five values that are very important for you and try to be as detailed as possible. For example, if you start off by writing down 'peace' you can expand it by explaining that not only do you value inner peace within yourself, but you also expect to build and maintain peaceful relationships with your loved ones.

The most beautiful thing about acknowledging your values is that not only are they going to remind you that you deserve to live an honest and fulfilling life, but they are also going to help you construct that strong and courageous voice you've been yearning for.

Question 3: Do You Believe in Limits?

Now that you've had enough time to think about your limiting beliefs, it's time to write them down. Think about three strong and destructive limiting beliefs that have been haunting you and blocking you from moving forward in your life. They could've come from your parents, your peers, school, or even from yourself.

When writing them down, start with the word "I" and use the present tense. For example, you could say "I am so loud it makes people uncomfortable," or "I am selfish," or "I'll never get the job I want."

Then, modify these sentences by making them as optimistic as possible, even if you don't believe them. So, you'll now have: "I have a strong voice that grabs people's attention," "I like to put myself first," and "I know I'm good enough to get the job I've always dreamed of."

What you just did is create statements that are going to challenge your negative thoughts and help you avoid the destructive patterns that have been limiting you; these statements are called affirmations.

Positive affirmations are quite powerful; they will help you gain a positive outlook of yourself, help you believe in yourself more, and enable you to resist any threats that are going to make you undervalue yourself!

Research shows that affirmations rewire the brain by influencing our neural pathways (Cascio et al., 2015). This means that whenever you verbalize them, your brain begins to understand how important that statement is to you and because you will be constantly putting the statement at the core of your conscious and unconscious level, you are more likely to start taking definitive action to make the affirmation true. So, with the statements above, you will notice yourself gaining the courage to speak up more with authority, you'll put yourself first, and work smarter to get your dream job.

The only action plan for this question is that you will need to connect with your inner self by including these affirmations in your daily routine.

Start off slowly by committing to declaring them three to five times a day. You could use one of the affirmations in the morning, another in the afternoon, and the third one just before you go to bed. Say them with conviction, and repeat them as often as it suits you.

The first few days are going to be uncomfortable, but with time, you will start to notice the difference through the actions you are going to take.

Question 4: What Are Your Strengths?

It's easy to talk about the things we're bad at or how many times we've failed, but we should also make a habit of identifying our strengths so that we can learn to take advantage of them too!

Take the opportunity to list five things that you believe you're good at. It could be anything from cooking to fixing appliances, or even time management. The aim here is to help you realize just how unique and amazing you are.

There are so many benefits to finding your inner strengths. One of the most important benefits is that once you become aware of who you are and how worthy you are of all the things you've always wanted, you will gain the courage to pick yourself up no matter how many times you fall.

For example, knowing that you are good at your job is what will drive you to go and advocate for better working conditions, no matter how scared you are to initiate that discussion. Obstacles are part of life; your strengths are going to help you conquer them.

Question 5: Do You Remember When?

You might be feeling a little less powerful, confident, and courageous now, but that does not mean there was never a time when you weren't.

This last question requires you to write about your past successes, to remind yourself that if you could do it then, you're going to be able to do it now and in the future.

Think of three instances where you succeeded at something. Remember success is personal; so, don't feel foolish by listing things that aren't dramatic and big. It could be as simple as changing a negative situation you never thought you'd be able to, achieving something at school, or that one time you saved your colleague from making a costly mistake at work.

The beauty about all of these questions and the answers you've given is that they can (and should) always be revisited. Every time you face an obstacle refer to question five to remind yourself that you're capable of success.

You can use the answers to any of these questions as your affirmations to alter the way you think and kick out the negative thoughts that have been slowing you down all along.

Congratulations, you have gotten to know yourself a little better!

Step 2: Show Yourself Love and Care

So, what do self-love and self-care have to do with assertiveness? Well, the answer lies in the fact that people tend to treat you how you treat yourself. If you can master being aware of how you treat yourself, then you are more likely to start getting the treatment and things you've always wanted from life and those around you.

Below are a few things that you can do to start valuing yourself more and ultimately teach others how to treat you too.

Surround Yourself With Positivity

When you choose to surround yourself with people who constantly remind you of your shortcomings, you will fail to move forward and make positive changes in your life. These people could also be problem-oriented, meaning that instead of finding solutions to problems, they prefer to dwell on all the things that are going wrong and why things will never change for them.

However, if you spend more time with optimistic and solution-oriented people, you'll find yourself adopting the positive energy that they carry. Meaning you'll start to see yourself differently, copy and apply the methods that they use to solve problems, and also have a whole different view of yourself and life in general. Think about the people who are draining you and ask yourself whether you still want to continue spending time with them.

Be Kind to Yourself

This sounds cliche, but no one is perfect. You're a unique human being but you are also flawed and have made some mistakes along the way. Nevertheless, you shouldn't hold on to your past mistakes and failures; this will only slow you down.

Instead, every time you think about the wrong choices you've made in your life, grab your journal and write about the incident. Give details of why these mistakes still haunt you but most importantly, reflect on the lessons you've learned from them. Ask difficult questions like *what could I have done better? Why did things go wrong?* Then identify the three most important lessons you've learned.

Self-reflection is a powerful tool that allows you to be better prepared for a situation that might present itself to you more than once. When you fail at something once, you are able to take in the mistakes you've made and then find ways you could avoid them the second time around. In this way, you'll avoid sabotaging yourself and will also find it easier to forgive yourself more quickly because you've acknowledged the errors that you've made.

Nevertheless, there's no point in identifying new ways of approaching a situation if you're not going to put them into practice. That's why it's important to develop an action plan that is going to make it hard for you to fail. For example, let's say you struggle with forgetfulness. You know you're a good listener, and you're able to take instructions well, but if you don't execute what is expected of you immediately, there is just no way that you're going to be able to complete your given tasks. This has gotten you into trouble a few times with your superiors and you can't help but to beat yourself about it. So, now that you know that forgetfulness is a major problem for you, how are you going to deal with it? Are you going to make notes every time you're given instruction, attend to the tasks immediately, or ask for help from your colleagues so that you never fail at completing a task again? Protecting yourself is a form of self-love and you should always use it to your advantage.

One of the most valuable things about continuously engaging in this exercise is that it will show you how far you've come as a flawed and unique individual. It will also help you gain the confidence to value yourself more and ultimately forgive yourself once and for all!

Step Three: Learn to Take Risks

Nobody tells you about the multiple times that they've failed; they only highlight the times that they've been successful. In order for you to achieve anything, you've got to be willing to take risks.

Of course, it's always nerve-wracking to put yourself in a position like that, but remember that the worst that could happen has probably already happened. When you decide to take a risk, you become intentional about what you want in your life and that is a beautiful thing.

Below are a few guidelines on how you can take risks and finally get what you want.

Make Calculated Risks

In essence, a risk is something that has the potential to expose you to danger and that is probably why you would rather play it safe. However, why don't you assess the level of the risk by making a list of all the challenges you'll face, the pros and cons of your decision, and how you will manage it should you fall into danger?

This type of strategy is what will move you from taking an ordinary risk to taking what is called a "calculated risk," an option that still has the potential to expose you to danger but is much safer because you have prepared for it.

Step Out of Your Comfort Zone

This is actually easier than you think!

Look at where you are in life right now and think about where you are trying to go. What changes do you need to make that will move you to live the life you've been dreaming of?

Your changes don't even have to be dramatic. You could ask for more responsibility at work if you are trying to get a promotion, enroll in an activity that you've always wanted to try out, or commit to breaking a habit that is hindering you from being bold.

Not only will you make progress in your life, but you will also gain more confidence in yourself, as you will be reclaiming your power to live the life you've always wanted.

Make a Suggestion

Suggestions may sound risky if you fear that you'll be ignored. Keep in mind it's just an idea that you're asking someone to consider. You know they could say "no," but they could also say "yes" and start valuing your opinion more

They will also get to understand what kind of perspective you take to tackle situations and might get a hint of what your needs are.

Chapter 3:

Transform Your Communication Skills

I encourage people to remember that "no" is a complete sentence. –Gavin de Becker

Oh, don't you just envy your colleague who always manages to get their points across fluently and confidently? Do you wish you could have the ability to say "no" and walk away without feeling guilty about it? Better yet, do you wish you could simply stop saying "sorry" every minute of the day?

Communication is more than just about the ability to relay and receive information, its ultimate goal lies in a person being able to be heard and having their concepts carried out. When you are on a mission to gain more assertiveness in your life, your main goal should be to express yourself clearly in a calm manner and also to walk away from a conversation knowing that your wishes will be respected and carried out. It's not always easy to achieve this because irrespective of who you're engaging with in a conversation, you both want to walk away satisfied. When you are not assertive, you are more likely to feel drained by the need to express yourself and will end up compromising your needs for them.

Let's look at this on a more practical level. A friend of yours insists that you should go on a vacation. While the trip might be tempting, you know there is no way you can afford to go out for a weekend so abruptly, and unsurprisingly, some of your other friends have expressed the same sentiments too. However, this particular friend of yours is oblivious to this and seems so excited that she even started looking for posh hotels for you and your girls. Given this scenario, you have three ways to respond to it:

1. You tell your friend that you don't have a problem with going on the trip, despite knowing very well that you shouldn't even be entertaining this proposal. In your mind, you start thinking about borrowing some money from a family member because you don't want to disappoint your friend.
2. In a clear and calm manner, you let your friend know that although you'd be happy to join her on the trip, you just don't have enough money.
3. You argue with your friend and tell her she's selfish and inconsiderate for forcing you to go on this trip. As the conversation continues to heat up, you storm out of the room and don't look back!

If you're reading this book, there's a chance you won't respond the second way. However, if you believe you could, then you already possess some of the qualities of an assertive communicator. Assertive communicators are people who are both honest and empathetic. Although they respect all opinions and remain calm and polite throughout a conversation, they are able to speak their minds and have their wishes respected.

If you think you'd respond in the first way then you're a passive communicator. This means that you always intend to keep the peace by keeping your heartfelt opinions to yourself and will agree with everything that another person has to say, as long as it will help you avoid conflict or confrontation.

If you believe you'd respond in a third way then you're an aggressive communicator, one who is concerned about speaking your mind as loud as you can and with little or no consideration about how another person might feel.

As a woman who aspires to be bold and courageous, it's important that you know the type of communicator you are so that you can work on your skills. You see, these scenarios are always going to present themselves, whether it's at work, home, or in your relationship. The only way you're going to know if you're truly assertive is by analyzing the way you respond to such requests.

Don't worry if you've identified yourself as an aggressive or passive communicator; communication is a skill that can be improved and mastered. This chapter will teach your five main ways to improve your communication. The steps to become a master communicator include:

1. Adapting your vocabulary
2. Discovering words to avoid
3. Learning how to say "no"
4. Confidently accepting compliments
5. Knowing when and how to apologize

How to Adapt Your Vocabulary

On your quest to become an assertive speaker, your first task is going to be making changes to your everyday vocabulary.

Of course, some people take advantage of us because they know we are passive and we are going to agree to whatever they say to us—no matter how uncomfortable we are. However, it's also important to note that people are not mind readers, so they won't know if we're uncomfortable with something unless we express it to them. The power to be taken advantage of, made uncomfortable, or oppressed, lies in our vocabulary!

Say "I…"

Because the lack of assertiveness stems from the need to put other people first, you should start by using the word "I" more often.

Remember that you are trying to take control of your life and should therefore aim to put yourself first. By beginning your sentence with "I" you gain power by letting the individual on the receiving end know exactly what you think or how you feel. This also prevents you from sounding too judgmental because your sentence will be giving a clear indication that your response is centered around your needs, and has nothing to do with them.

For example, there is a huge difference between "I would like you to help with the laundry" and "You need to do the laundry" or "I don't think I'll be able to go" and "You want me to be there." The "I" sentences clearly convey what you want from a situation while the "You" sentence makes it clear that it's always about the other person. The more you use sentences that speak to your needs, the more people will know that you value yourself and they should too!

To construct a sentence that is going to put you first, you should begin by doing the following:

1. Listen or think about what is being requested or done: Why does it make you uncomfortable or resistant?
2. Keep a mental note of how the other person feels and what they have communicated or done.
3. Think about what you want.

From these points, you should be able to create a constructive response. For example, you have a dilemma with a roommate who smokes in your apartment whenever you're not around. This makes you uncomfortable because you are conscious about your health and simply hate the smell that lingers everywhere around your space.

Your roommate only smokes in the house when you're not around, which means they could either be aware of the fact that what they're doing is wrong, or they believe they are being polite by only doing it when you're not around.

Irrespective of what their reason could be, you want to let them know that you don't want them to smoke in the house. So, you could end up saying to them "Roommate, I respect your decision to smoke, but is there a way you could do it outside?" or "Roommate, I noticed that you may be smoking in the house. I'd really appreciate it if you could rather do it outside."

The aim should be to keep the sentence

- Concise enough for the receiver to understand your position or request.
- Reflective so that the receiver may know you mean no harm and understand where they're coming from. More often than not, when you show your receiver that

you've thought about the situation, you give them an opportunity to also think about their actions or words.
- Personal, because it's actually about you!

Depending on the situation, sometimes you don't even have to give an explanation, but relevant questions enable you to start a conversation and also make the other party aware that there are other options that they could explore. For example, the scenario about the roommate who smokes in the house could end up with a conversation where they tell you that they had no idea that you were bothered by it, or they could tell you that they never thought of using the balcony because they don't have the keys to the sliding door.

Starting your sentences with "I" is not going to be easy or happen overnight. Therefore, you should start practicing it by thinking of scenarios where you could use it to your advantage. Think about the situation and apply the three points that are going to help you construct your sentence.

Formulate as many scenarios as you can and practice your answers as often as you can. The more you do this, the more you will gain the confidence to put yourself through the simple act of saying "I."

Words Assertive Women Don't Use

You should know that once you join the "elite club of assertive women," there are certain words you should never utter from your precious lips.

Women don't know this, but they often sabotage themselves by using sentences that scream "I won't blame you for doubting me, I doubt me too!" The most surprising thing about these words or sentences is that they use them in their everyday speech, meaning that they make it common knowledge that they struggle with boldness and displaying courage.

Below are five words you should get rid of as in yesterday!

1. The use of qualifiers

"I'm no expert but…" "This might be a silly idea but…" or "I know this might be a stupid question but…"

Why are you letting the world know that you're no expert? Why do you belittle yourself so much that you think your brain is full of silly thoughts? And darling, there's no such thing as a stupid question!

Tara Mohr, a career and personal growth coach, always advises her female clients to stop using undermining qualifiers in their speech and writing, and the results are always unbelievable! "I get so many emails from women who are excited to share with me how people responded to them differently. Many women—especially more junior women—share that when they took all the qualifiers out of their emails, they started getting much quicker and more substantive responses to their requests" (n.d., para. 10).

This is a clear indication that if you don't take yourself seriously, no one else will.

2. The "check-in" conclusion

"Does that make sense?" "Do you get what I'm trying to say?"

This sentence creates an opportunity for you to show the whole world that you are probably not credible and are not convinced by what you're saying.

An assertive woman knows exactly what she's talking about and does not carry the responsibility of ensuring that you understand what she's saying. Once you have clearly put your point across, conclude your sentence by inviting a response "I hope to hear from you soon" or "I trust you are following me" are words you should start using.

3. "I'm sorry."

Did you know that women say sorry about ten times a day? This means they'll say it about 295,650 times in their lifetime (Freedman, 2019).

Why are you apologizing if you haven't done anything wrong? Remember that every time you do this, you hurt your self-esteem because you downplay your strengths, true intentions, and it makes you look like you're trying to appear likable.

Assertive women only apologize when they've done something wrong. So, the next time you ask a question or make a statement, begin your sentence with something other than apologizing.

4. "Just"

"I just wanted to know if…" and "I just thought I should…"

Please 'just' drop this word because it makes you sound defensive and apologetic for anything you've got to say after that. You don't have to be defensive or look down on your thoughts and opinions.

How powerful is "I think we should go with the red car" as opposed to "I just think we should go with the red car"? Yes, there is more strength in the first sentence!

5. Try

"I'll try to get it done by…" "I tried to…but…"

'Try' is a word that implies you might not be compatible with a task or responsibility. Every time you use this word, you give people the idea that they might've taken a chance by trusting you with something they could've easily given to someone. It's a word that is associated with doubt and should never be used if you're trying to prove you're good enough for something.

It's even worse when you use this word in the past tense because not only are you establishing doubt, but you're also saying your completed tasks had a great chance of not being delivered because you faced difficulties. Such suggestions will make another person think someone else could've been better suited for the responsibility.

Assertive women don't 'try' to do something. It's either they do something or they don't, and even when they decide to do it, they are going to deliver excellent results! This does not mean that you should never doubt yourself or become nervous when faced with challenging tasks, those are normal feelings that even the most successful people go through. However, successful people don't put it out there that they're nervous or doubtful of themselves, they tackle situations head-on because they know they've got a point to prove to themselves. This is an attitude you should start adopting instantly.

How to Say "No"

"No" is a word with just two letters but is so impactful it could end relationships or transform situations. It is the only word that proves whether you have power over a situation or not, and to be quite frank, if you can't use it in your life, then it suggests someone else has control over it.

There are a lot of effective ways that you can say no without feeling guilty. Below are a few methods that you should start using in your conversations.

"No" With a Reason

When you're an active listener during a discussion, you'll be able to reflect on a few points that will indicate to you that you should not be in agreement with what another person is saying. It then becomes your responsibility to say "no" but your refusal will not be effective if it does not come with a reason.

This doesn't mean that you should be explaining yourself; however, some people can walk away satisfied from a conversation if they are given an explanation or a reason behind your decision.

Let's go back to the example we made about going on a trip with your friends. You've established that you can't go because it was planned abruptly and you don't have the money for it. On your side, you should plan to have a constructive answer by giving a reason why you can't go on the trip. Remember that while your friend was telling you about the trip, you had enough time to draw reasons why you cannot go on the trip and that should be communicated to your friend.

You'll have to wait for them to finish talking to show that you were listening to them all along, and when it's your turn to finally talk, you should take a deep breath and give them your answer.

With all of this in mind, you can come up with an answer like this: "Friend, while I understand how this trip is important to you and our friendship, I'm afraid I'm going to have to say no because I feel like the vacation was planned at the last minute. I know I'll not be able to afford it."

This is an effective answer because it is accommodated by a valid reason and not an excuse. Finally, it contains emotive language like "feel," "understand," and "I'm afraid." After all, you were genuinely tempted to go on the trip and your friend has the right to know this too.

While you may not be in control of how they will respond, you should feel relieved because this type of response will leave little to no room for your friend to get upset as you would've been calm, clear, and respectful throughout.

The Broken Record Method

According to established Author Robert Bolton, this is a simple, powerful, and dramatic method that is guaranteed to give you control over a difficult and persistent individual.

Think about the calls we often receive from salesmen. From the minute you answer your phone, they are on a mission to convince you to buy something. No matter how many times you try to decline their offer, they always have an answer for you. It could be tempting to give in and sign up for their products, but this is probably the only time you are able to stick to your "no." When it comes to your friends, family, or colleagues though, you find it difficult to say no because you have some kind of emotional attachment or you fear disappointing them. So, you are often quick to comply but that is something you can learn to avoid using this effective method.

Let's continue with the example about the trip. No matter how many times you shrug or give an excuse, your friend keeps on telling you about how wonderful the trip will be. She tells you about the available activities, the fancy hotel you'll be staying in, and the great time that you're going to have. It's so easy to give in and end up going on that trip, but you should remember the valid reasons why you shouldn't even be entertaining that thought.

Unfortunately, when you find yourself dealing with persistent people like this, you will have to put in the same kind of persistence otherwise they are going to overpower you before you even know it!

This is how you can apply the broken record method:

1. Remember it's about you and what you want: Settle on a sentence you're going to use throughout the conversation. Do not overthink it, your sentence should just be concise, such as: "I cannot go on the trip."
At this point, your friend is going to try as hard as they can to persuade you and might even manipulate you with emotive language. "But friend, you know how much I need this trip, you've got to come with me!"
2. Remain calm and repeat your line. "I cannot go on the trip.

At this point, they might switch from manipulating you to becoming defensive and a bit irritated. "But why? It's not like we'll be gone for a week."
3. Repeat your sentence, this time with conviction. You might even want to close your eyes to remain calm or focused, or you might turn around and look them in the eyes to show them how serious you are. "I cannot go on the trip."

It's during this stage that your friend will become silent as they try to adjust to your stance. It is very important to allow this silence to go on for as long as it will. You see, this gives them enough time to think about how they are approaching this situation and they will finally come to the realization that their manipulations will be futile.

You should expect your friend to respond with annoyance and displeasure but this does not mean that you have to entertain them. Their disapproval of your decision is based on what they expected you to do or say and not how or what you really decided on. Give them time to deal with your decision but do not consider changing your mind. Whether they walk away, stop talking to you for a few days, or simply conclude the conversation with a blunt "fine," you should pat yourself on the shoulder for speaking your mind and keep it moving. More often than not, they will come around and let go of the incident.

Furthermore, you would've made it clear that your opinion needs to be respected, even if it means you repeating it 500 times like an annoying broken record!

The Vigorous "No"

There are some situations and requests that don't require you to give a 'valid' reason. Your refusal to participate in something or agree with someone is a completely personal decision and everyone in your life should respect this. It's important to note though that this only becomes a viable option if trying to reflect or justify your answer is going to make the situation even more difficult for you. So, conclude your answer and the conversation with a flat-out "no."

When your response is met with great irritation and you are asked to give a reason, you could simply tell them that you don't have a reason but you believe your answer should be a no. It seems like a difficult task, but you won't look back after you try it out.

How to Accept Compliments for What They Are

Once you spend each and every day of your life criticizing the way you look, walk, or talk, it comes as a shock to you when someone suddenly says, "You have such lovely eyes," or "That was a great suggestion!" If you are going to be an assertive woman, then you should start getting used to hearing and receiving such compliments.

According to social psychologist Laura Brannon, all women, no matter how successful they are, struggle with accepting compliments (2016).

Successful women are driven by the need to appear modest while women with low self-esteem reject compliments because what they are told is inconsistent with the beliefs they have about themselves. This fear is so deep that when it is handed over to us, we immediately become anxious, freeze as our faces turn red, and then ultimately save ourselves from the dreadful ordeal by steering the conversation in a different direction. We've all done it, someone will tell you that your hair looks good and you'll deflect the statement by letting them know how painful it was to get it done. They'll tell you they love how you solved a problem at work, and you'll tell them that your other colleague is actually the one who came in and saved you. It's a terrible habit to have, but it is completely understandable.

Why You Should Accept Compliments

When someone takes the effort to say something nice about you, they actually mean it. When you make the situation worse by choosing to reject it, you force them to wonder why they made the effort in the first place. Secondly, you make things awkward because you are going to spend the next few minutes trying to reject another compliment. Think about it, when someone tells you that an outfit looks good on you, you might be tempted to respond by saying "Oh, but I hate that it highlights my long arms." This instantly forces the other person to come up with a reason why your long arms actually look good in that outfit. You can avoid this awkwardness by simply saying "Thank you!"

Secondly, people don't spend a lot of time over-analyzing and criticizing you the way you think they do.

In the same way that you choose to identify the things you like about someone the first time you see them, they obviously choose to do the same thing to you. Compliments are honest observations from people. Take them as they are and start realizing that you're an amazing woman who is recognized by the people around her!

How You Should Accept Compliments

Say "Thank You"

Do not overthink it, you should simply smile and say "thank you" or "thanks." Unfortunately, there is no other way around it! Of course, you are going to feel uncomfortable the first few times but you should tell yourself that it's a skill worth learning.

Affirm It

When the person who has complimented you leaves the room, affirm the compliment back to yourself as many times as you can. For example, if they tell you: "That dress suits you so beautifully!" You should tell yourself: "I'm so comfortable in my body that I deserve to have nice things said to me!" As you continue with this exercise, you'll begin to appreciate yourself for who you are and what you've got to offer to the world.

Pause…Reflect and Take It In!

It might seem strange but right after you've been given a compliment, pause and think about what has just been said to you. "Just take a breath and say to yourself, 'There's a person in the world who thinks I look fab today.' Then track how it makes you feel." (2015, para. 15) says psychotherapist and life coach Alyson Lanier. Reflecting on how good you feel every time someone recognizes you is what will build you and help you realize that you are worthy of the praises that come your way.

Taking in a compliment well will not happen overnight but please, for the sake of showing yourself some love, take the compliment because you truly deserve it!

Should You Apologize?

Yes, but only if you've wronged someone. The habit of apologizing for almost everything does more harm to you than good on a personal and professional level.

There are a lot of reasons why we fall into the ritual of over-apologizing. It could come from childhood trauma, the fear of hurting another person, and a need to nudge another person to apologize to you as well.

However, if you find yourself constantly apologizing without valid reasons then you run the risk of weakening future apologies. This is because the more you use the word in irrelevant situations, the more it will lose value, especially to the person who always receives it from you. In fact, they will think you say sorry as a quick fix to everything and cannot take accountability for your actions.

How Should You Stop Saying Sorry?

The only way you can stop over-using this word is by learning to substitute it with words that are relevant to a particular situation. These words include "excuse me" and "thank you."

If You're Running Late

The fact that you're late has already annoyed the people who have been waiting for you. Of course, they're expecting you to apologize but you could ease off the tension and show your gratitude by saying "Thank you for waiting for me."

If You're About to Interrupt Someone

It sounds a bit ridiculous to apologize for interrupting if you're going to interrupt the person anyway. It paints you as an ignorant person who is more concerned about talking than listening in a conversation. Instead of apologizing, you could use a sentence that gives a reason why you're interrupting the person in the first place. So, you could say, "I'd like to expand on what you're saying," or "I'd like to add on that." This proves that not only have you been listening to what they've been saying, but also that their points are so good they've sparked more ideas from you.

If You're About to Complain

Going on and on about something that makes you unhappy can drain the life out of the people who are listening to your rants.

Adding on the element of "I'm sorry" can be even more irritating because it genuinely does not solve the situation.

No one wants to listen to someone complain, instead of apologizing for doing it anyway. Adopt the habit of saying "thank you for listening to me," and your listener will appreciate your awareness of the situation.

In Emails

Don't you just cringe every time you open an email and the first thing you read is "Sorry?" There are chances you do this too!

If someone picks up an error and brings it to your attention, don't apologize for it. If the error is maintainable and does not affect the people around you, you should rather thank them for making you aware of it.

You could instead say "Thank you for bringing this to my attention," or "I appreciate you flagging this issue to me," and then find solutions to manage the problem. These types of lines will highlight you as someone who owns up to their mistakes, appreciates the people who bring them to their attention, and does not feel the need to apologize when there is simply no need.

When You're About to Ask or Answer a Question

You should not be apologizing for asking a question or having an answer to a question; it will only make you look like you're undermining yourself. Instead, get into the habit of reminding yourself why it's important to ask or answer the question. This will give you the confidence to go ahead and speak up, even when it feels 'scary.'

When You Can't Go to Work or Need Time Off

It's easy to feel guilty whenever you have to ask for time off from work. However, you can't apologize for falling ill or taking time off to be there for your family. No one wants to share their space with someone who might infect them, so not only will you come back feeling better, but your colleagues will thank you for saving them from falling ill too.

Furthermore, when your company awards you annual leave days, they do it because they know you've got to take time off to go and recharge. Take that time and don't feel guilty about it—you genuinely deserve a break.

When You Need Help

Instead of saying "Sorry to disturb you, but can you please help me," why don't you ask the person to help you at their convenience? So, you could say "I see you're still busy, can you please help me when you have time?"

There is nothing wrong with asking for help, especially if the person you're asking has not even complained yet.

When You Need to Express Yourself or How You're Feeling

"I'm sorry but I don't agree…" or "I'm sorry this might upset you but…"

Your feelings and views are relevant, if you use statements like these, you give people the impression that you are doubtful of what you're thinking or feeling and that they shouldn't take you seriously. Don't allow such thoughts to cross people's minds. If you want to express yourself freely, do it the right way by believing in what you're saying.

Transforming your communication skills by trading in unnecessary words, believing in what you're saying, and putting yourself first is the only way you can take your power back.

Unfortunately, the exercises in this chapter cannot be practiced in your journal only. You will have to practice them in your everyday conversations with real humans! There is no doubt that you're going to struggle the first few times you begin your sentences with "I" or are prompted to say "no," but communication is an effective skill that can be improved and mastered.

Try these strategies with people you feel comfortable with, and then gradually move them to the people who need to hear you say these words the most.

For example, if you're more comfortable around your mother and she is aware of your desire to gain more assertiveness, you could ask her to help you practice the exercises in the chapter. Say "no" to her, thank her for waiting for you, and accept the compliments she gives you.

Then, when you're finally ready to take your newfound skills to the world, do it with conviction. Remain unshaken and remind yourself that the worst that could happen is what has been happening anyway. You need to find your power, you need to speak out for yourself, and people need to know how you feel and what you want. Communication is the only thing that will get you all of these things!

Chapter 4:

Setting and Keeping Healthy Boundaries

Your personal boundaries protect the inner core of your identity and your right to choices. —Gerard Manley Hopkins

When I was in my 20s I worked with this older and much more experienced sales guy who was very nice but quite sexist, even though I don't think he was aware of it. We would be sitting in a sales meeting with a potential client and he'd say something patronizing like "Run along and get coffees for us." It really bothered me, to say the least.

I kept going over in my mind how to tackle this and one day, I gained the courage to finally speak up and said, "Jim when you say things like 'go get the coffee' it makes me feel small and subordinate instead of your equal" (which I was).

It was quite an incredible scene as I watched his jaw drop after I said it. Although I delivered it as nicely as I could, he still took it quite badly at the time but never did it again. I don't know if I could've handled this better but the mere act of gaining the courage to set a boundary made me feel assertive and left me with the desired effect that I've been craving for such a long time.

In its simplest form, a personal boundary refers to what you consider to be acceptable or unacceptable behavior toward you. Oftentimes, we know how we want to be treated, but we struggle communicating this to the people we interact with.

Boundaries exist in our relationships, physical spaces, and even in the digital space. For example, you are allowed to tell your partner that although you're in an exclusive relationship with them, you don't feel comfortable sharing your relationship on social media. Boundaries are all about setting healthy limitations in your relationships because you want to be comfortable.

Why Do You Need Boundaries?

Imagine if you could walk into your favorite store right now. As you're doing your shopping, someone tells you that for today only, you can walk away with as many items as you want. There are no limits, and no terms or conditions, and you won't even have to pay a single dime for your items. What would you do?

Of course, you wouldn't even think twice. You're going to grab things you've always wanted to buy but couldn't afford. You'd also think of your loved ones and start taking things they'd want. I imagine you'd walk carefully, aisle by aisle, making sure to not miss a single thing. What was meant to be a 30-minute trip to the shops will turn into a three-hour extravaganza.

Believe it or not, this is how people approach you in life. Once they find out that you don't really have a lot of terms and conditions on how you want to be treated, they will walk into your life and take as much as they can from you. When you don't speak out about this, they will enjoy this kind of treatment and even start using you to advance in their own lives.

As an assertive woman, you need to have boundaries set in your life. Not only are they an indication of self-respect and self-care, but they also give people an indication of how you want to be treated in your life.

Women who don't have boundaries often struggle to identify their own needs and emotions and ultimately end up being overly sensitive to people's criticisms. They are unable to protect themselves from being hurt and repeatedly find themselves in situations where they are taken advantage of just because they simply do not have limits. If you do not have boundaries, you will never feel safe in your life because just about anyone can step into your personal space and take anything that they want from you.

Today they'll ask you for some money, then they'll ask to borrow your car before they finally move into your house for free. At work, you could find yourself helping someone out with a small favor, and before you know it, you'll be putting in an extra hour or two because they just need you to urgently fill in for them. How are you going to stop them when you've made it so clear that you're okay with this? You've never said "no" or questioned their intentions; you've just been filling in for everyone because well, you have no boundaries.

When you set boundaries, you let people know that you expect them to behave in a certain way. Once they do not meet your expectations, you can gauge where you stand in their lives and what exactly they think of you, and the relationship that you have. Of course, you're not going to eliminate them from your life, but it gives you an opportunity to have a conversation.

Now that you're convinced of the importance of boundaries, it's time to figure out what yours are and how to keep them. You'll do this by following these steps:

1. Identifying your boundaries
2. Communicating your boundaries
3. Responding when your boundaries are challenged
4. Learning self-care to maintain your boundaries

Step One: Identify and Name Your Boundaries

Before you can show or tell people how to treat you, you need to know what your boundaries are.

In order to pick them out, imagine a boundary as a line that separates you from the rest of the whole world. This particular line cannot be moved or adjusted by anyone except yourself. On the one side of the line is your personal space: This is where you can be free and live life on your own terms. If anyone decides to come into your space, they need to respect and adjust to these terms otherwise you'll have to call them out.

The first step to respecting your personal space is by identifying what your values are and then combining them with the terms you have set for your life.

What do you consider to be acceptable or unacceptable in your personal and professional relationships? Take this as an opportunity for you to connect with your emotions and make a conscious decision to honor them. Grab your journal and pinpoint ten things that you will allow and ten things you consider unacceptable in your relationships and your workplace environment.

Step Two: Communicate Your Boundaries

Setting boundaries can be quite intimidating because up until now, you've never been able to properly communicate your wants and needs. The only way to make people aware of how you want to be treated is by communicating your limits to them.

Depending on the nature of the relationship, boundaries can be communicated anywhere and at any time, as long as it's done calmly and respectfully. For example, in your romantic relationship, your partner has this habit of always showing up at your house unannounced. Once they're there, they expect you to spend time with them, which often means you'd have to drop all your plans for the day.

The next time they do this, you can gently tell them that you believe they should call you before they come to your house to check your availability so you can avoid getting disappointed. A healthy relationship should always be open to conversations about boundaries, limits, and expectations.

Looking at my story with Jim, you remember that I didn't schedule a meeting with him to let him know about his unacceptable behavior. I simply said it as pleasantly as I could. However, that may not always be the case when you have to discuss serious matters with your manager or with someone from HR. The aim is to look at the nature of the relationship and the situation at hand before you can address your boundaries. Irrespective of this, you should be able to communicate your boundaries.

Step Three: When Your Boundaries Are Challenged

How should you react when someone crosses your boundaries? You should be assertive and let them know about it. Your boundaries are practically worthless if you cannot enforce them and exercise consequences for anyone who will cross them.

People generally like to challenge boundaries, so once you put them out there, expect them to be questioned and defied. How many times has your friend who doesn't respect your time told you "Relax, I'm just late by five minutes" when you've tried to tell them countless times that it's not really about being late, it's about respecting your time?

The only way you put an end to this is if you sit them down and make them understand where you're coming from.

Below are a few guidelines you should follow when you want your boundaries to be respected:

1. **Make sure the time is right**

Timing is everything! Picking the right time to speak about a serious matter is a crucial part of guaranteeing the possibility of a successful conversation.

You should aim to choose a date and time that will be convenient for both you and the other party. Remember that you won't be the only one doing the talking, so ensure that you'll have enough time to have an exhaustive conversation.

2. Choose a convenient place

Make sure the environment where your discussion will be held is private and neutral enough for the other party not to feel like they're being attacked.

If you're having this conversation with a friend, maybe pick a place that you know they like. This will ease off the tension that might build up while you're having the discussion and will make your friend realize that you have nothing but good intentions.

3. Invite the person to the conversation

There is a big emotional difference between "We need to talk right now," versus "May we talk about what happened earlier," or "I'd like to chat to you about a few thoughts and feelings that I have."

Regardless of what might've transpired between you and your friend or colleague, it's always a good idea to show them that you still have respect for them by inviting them to the conversation instead of demanding their attention.

When you extend your invitation, make it clear that you are interested in having a conversation and what the conversation will be about.

Finally, ask them about their availability so they won't feel like they're being forced to urgently attend to your petition.

4. Express yourself

Going into the conversation, you should have three things in mind: your thoughts, feelings, and the person's behavior.

Then, think about the power of beginning your sentence with "I." This is your moment to put yourself first, use it!

After beginning your sentence with "I," you can establish your thoughts or feelings and then include the person's behavior, before finally ending the sentence with your thoughts or feelings again. Remember that all of the elements need to be included in the sentence. If you begin with your thoughts, you'll have to end with your feelings.

For example, let's reconstruct my exchange with Jim using the guideline above. My sentence for that day would have either been:

- I feel disrespected (feeling) when you order me around (person's behavior) because I think as your equal, there's definitely a better way of speaking to me. (thought). Alternatively, you could apply a positive twist to it and say, "I'd really appreciate it if you could stop talking to me like that, especially in front of potential clients. I'm your equal Jim, and that should be enough to encourage you to give me the same level of respect that I give you."
- I think you should find better ways of talking to me (thought) because I feel disrespected when you order me around (feeling), especially in the presence of potential clients (person's behavior).

However, note that these are not the only ways that you can express yourself. Of course, some situations won't follow this guideline to the tee, but it's key to understand the power of those three elements combined in your discussion.

5. Listen

While the conversation is going to be about communicating your boundaries, you still need to remember that it takes two to make any kind of relationship work. You would be surprised to learn that the other person was completely unaware that they've overstepped your boundaries and that they meant no harm.

The beautiful thing about boundaries is that everyone has them, although they don't necessarily communicate them as clearly as they should. So, it's your responsibility to respect their boundaries as well by listening and trying to see things from their perspective.

This does not mean that you need to compromise what you're feeling, because "being willing to admit your own wrongdoings and owning your mistakes is a sign of emotional maturity that will strengthen and sustain your relationships" (Hanks, 2016, p. 170).

6. Embrace their reaction:

It does not matter whether they will resent you, walk away, or simply stop talking to you for a while, as long as you have communicated your needs, then you've done a good job for yourself. There will always be a time to cool off after a difficult heart-to-heart, so don't take their reaction personally, they will be just reacting to the fact that you've started putting yourself first.

No matter how tempting it'll be for you to reach out, allow them to take in the content of your discussion, and once they've cooled off and reached out to you, embrace their comeback and work on rebuilding your relationship with them.

It's going to hurt should they decide to walk away and completely cut you off, but think about it this way: Do you really want to keep people who don't respect your boundaries in your life?

As difficult as it might be to deal with the end of your relationship with that person, in the long run, you'll realize or accept that it was never going to work anyway. They simply don't want you to live life on your own terms and that is not fair for you or your well-being.

Step Four: Practice Self-Care and Make Time For You!

Part of setting healthy boundaries for yourself includes occasionally dedicating some uninterrupted time to yourself.

Have you noticed how people have this odd habit of jumping into your personal space without even feeling guilty about it?

Think about that one friend who always calls you and doesn't bother to ask if it's a good time to talk. They go on and on about the problems they have and once they're done offloading, they finally ask how you're doing before hanging up like they don't even care how you're really doing.

When you can't give yourself time to recharge and focus on yourself, how are you going to have the energy to live your life the way you really want to? You can't pride yourself as being the friend, family member, or colleague "who's always there" for people but can barely make time for herself.

Have a Schedule and Stick to It

On a personal note, you should be able to tell how much time you're willing to give people without feeling like you're making an overwhelming sacrifice.

Think about phone calls, night outs, and time you spend "being there" for people. Can you honestly say you're putting yourself first? Chances are, your answer is "no." You can fix this by creating a personal schedule that prioritizes carving out time for yourself.

Look at all aspects of your life and investigate how much time you're willing to give, and where you will begin to draw boundaries.

In your calendar, think about completely blocking off certain days; no one should be able to steal this time from you. When you block it off, write down what you intend to do on that day so that you can become proactive in making it happen.

Do you want to spend the whole day in bed catching up on your favorite TV show? Will you spend half of the day reading a book and then sleep for the rest of the day? Whatever activity you think of getting up to, write it down, and make sure it happens!

Limit Phone Interactions

The next time your friend calls, establish it very early in the call that you only have five minutes to talk as you are in the middle of something. You will notice how they are going to summarize their conversation and give you the precious time that you need to yourself.

Maybe you struggle with texting throughout the day. Let your recipient know from the beginning that they should expect delayed responses from you as you are busy with something else.

The sooner you let them know that your time is limited, the easier it'll be for them to respect it by getting to the point and leaving you alone as soon as they're done!

Working Overtime

From the moment you show your superiors and colleagues at work that you're always available to work overtime or help out here and there, they will take advantage of it. This will leave you feeling drained and undervalued.

Maybe you don't mind working a few extra shifts, so decide to settle on doing it twice a month. Have a conversation with your manager about this by stating why you are no longer able to work on all weekends. Although it's not necessary to over-explain yourself, you could tell them that you'd appreciate it if they could give you an opportunity to spend more time with your family or rest more so that you can start being more productive again.

Use phrases like "I'd really like to, but now is not a good time for me" or simply state that your current life circumstances or commitments do not allow you to work as much as you used to before.

Furthermore, you could also spark a conversation about working smarter and not harder. If you're supposed to work five days a week but you're asked to come in on some weekends, ask your manager if there's a way you could do some of your weekend work during the week. You'll find that sometimes you don't even have to spend an extra day doing work that could be squeezed in or delegated to your other team members during the week.

Don't Always Be Reachable

When you feel like your work follows you everywhere you go, check if you've made yourself excessively reachable. For example, you should consider reading and responding to your emails only during your working hours. As soon as you get home, make a conscious decision to be available for your family by not checking your emails, or responding to requests outside of your working hours.

When someone from work calls during your family time, you need to be bold enough to let them know that you won't be able to attend to them.

Construct your response by letting them know why you can't attend to their request at that moment, and also provide an estimated time of when you will be able to get to it. Make sure this given time is within your working hours! So, you could say "I can't attend to that right now as I'm feeding my child, but I'll get to it first thing in the morning." Not only will this help you indicate that you're also dedicated to your life outside of work, but you are also assuring them that you won't completely neglect the task at hand.

In Your Relationships

Have you found yourself carrying your baby, preparing dinner for the family, and also tidying up the house while your partner is sitting and watching TV? It can be quite upsetting but you can't always blame them if you haven't communicated your desire to get a break to them.

Speak to your partner and ask them to start helping around the house. Maybe they should hold the baby more or help tidy up the house while you prepare dinner. Being able to delegate responsibilities more around the house is what will help you have more time to yourself.

Some friends always expect you to jump in and be there for them the minute they reach out to you. While it is a beautiful trait to have as a friend, you can't always put them first.

For example, your friend could ask you to pick them up from their house and drop them somewhere because they have transportation issues. Let's say you don't mind dropping them off but have a problem with having to wait for them to finish their appointment before going to drop them at home again.

Before you even fetch them, let your friend know that although you'd be glad to take them to their appointment, you simply cannot wait for them that long because you had prior commitments. If you can put your friend's needs first, you should show yourself some love by prioritizing your commitments as well!

Always Make Suggestions

Sometimes people need help finding solutions to their problems. For example, when your friend asks you to drive her to her appointment, suggest that she use public transport instead. Or when your partner tells you that they won't be able to help around the house as you've asked, suggest that you hire a helper instead.

Whatever the situation is, draw your boundaries by letting people know that you are no longer willing to compromise on your personal time.

Suggestions will always show that although you are unable to show up for another person, you care enough to think of solutions that would be beneficial to them. Whether they accept your suggestion or not, you should be proud of yourself for making the suggestion.

Give a Strategic Response…Always!

Whether it's with your family, friends, or even your boss, always use a delayed response to make it known that you respect your time and they should think about doing it too.

Although this strategy requires you to pause before you respond, you should not hold off for too long before you get back to the person. Aim to acknowledge the person in real-time to indicate that you are confident in what you're saying, but you also respect their time. "Let me check my availability and get back to you as soon as I can."

In other words, do not say "yes" right away, but give a response that is going to let the other person know that you've got a schedule to stick to.

You'll notice that the next time they come to you, they'll begin by asking about your availability instead of jumping right into making their requests. That is exactly what you need from people: to acknowledge that you can't always be available for them.

The skill of identifying and setting boundaries is not something that will happen overnight. However, once you do it, you will earn the respect you deserve from others.

When working on your boundaries, remember to put yourself first, remain consistent even when you are challenged, and respect other people's boundaries too.

Chapter 5:

Regulate Emotions and Body Language

What you do speaks so loud that I cannot hear what you say. –Ralph Waldo Emerson

Did you know that according to Albert Mehrabian's 7-38-55 Communication model, 7% of communication is expressed through words, 38% is conveyed through vocal tone and volume, while a whopping 55% takes place through body language? (Masterclass staff, 2020).

This means that while you might struggle to tell people what you want or how you feel, it's your body posture, eye movement, gestures, and facial expressions that are going to give you away!

"There's evidence to suggest our brains prioritize nonverbal communication over verbal communication. So, when our brain gets a mixed message — say it hears, 'I love you' but sees a mean face, or hears an insincere tone — it may prefer the nonverbal cues to the verbal ones," says marriage and family therapist Dr. Emily Cook. (as cited in Raypole, 2020, para. 6).

In essence, nonverbal communication is a powerful language of feelings. How many times have you witnessed someone walk into a room bursting with confidence? Before they speak, you can tell by the way they walk, smile, and maintain eye contact that they know who they are and what they're about. In the same breath, you've also been aware of someone who was so uncomfortable that you thought they'd probably get up and run out of the room. It's the way they dressed, spoke so softly, and even struggled to complete a sentence that alerted you that they weren't confident of themselves.

The people above behaved in the manner that they did because they felt a certain way about themselves or the situation they found themselves in.

Although nonverbal communication is often expressed on an unconscious level, meaning you may not even be aware that you're using it to convey information about yourself, you should still be aware of the fact that it stems from an emotional place. Because of this, it's always important that you're able to regulate your feelings.

Author and licensed therapist Dr. Julie De Azevedo-Hanks says she likes to think of emotions as "E-motions" or energies-in-motion. (2016, p. 94). If you think about energy as an entity that is always on the move, you will begin to realize that your emotions are indeed an energy that indicates how you feel about yourself at any given time. This will trigger you to assert yourself in situations that make you uncomfortable.

This means that there are no 'right' or 'wrong' emotions. What you feel cannot be invalidated by anyone; however, it is always important to be able to regulate your feelings to attain favorable results.

In this chapter, we are going to explore the various ways in which we can use our emotions and body language to create positive changes in our lives. We can only do this by leveraging the power of reading people's body language and also regulating our own.

Let's Talk About Your Feelings

The whole point of being assertive stems from a need to have people understand how we feel. However, how are they going to know how we're feeling if we're not connected to our emotions? When you are aware of how a person or situation makes you feel, you are more likely to crave assertiveness than just react to the situation.

In the 1970s, Psychologist Paul Eckman identified six emotions that he argued were universal and common in all humans, these emotions are happiness, sadness, disgust, fear, surprise, and anger.

When you find yourself in a dangerous situation you'll admit being scared; after a heated argument with someone, you'll shout that you're angry; and when you're relieved things are finally going your way, you'll proudly announce how happy you are. These emotive descriptions are so common and overused that they somehow no longer have an impact. In order to fix this, you'll have to work on expanding your vocabulary.

Identify Your Emotions

For a very long time, we've always thought it'd be great for ourselves and others if we could simply compress our feelings or not talk about how we feel.

For the next seven days, work on expanding your vocabulary and identifying your feelings. At the end of each day, write about an emotionally charged incident that you encountered. It could be anything from being late for work to laughing out loud with a colleague during your lunch break—anything that triggered an emotional reaction from you.

The only restriction in this exercise is that you are not allowed to use any of the six commonly used emotive descriptions mentioned above. So, instead of using the word "happy," you could use "delighted" and instead of "disgust," you could use "distasteful" and so forth.

In your journal go through the following steps:

1. Begin by describing the incident. Where were you? Who were you with? And what transpired?
2. Reflect on how you felt at the beginning of the incident. Maybe you were motivated to get started on a task you've been putting off for a while before you received that dreadful phone call.
3. In one word, describe how you felt as soon as you answered the phone and received the bad news.
4. Are you aware of how your body reacted? This is also an important element that you should include. Maybe you remember your hands shaking at some point, or you threw your phone to the ground as soon as the bad news hit you. Write everything down.
5. Then, amplify your answer by focusing on the one word you used in the previous step. Let's say you settled on "shocked." What does this word mean to you?
6. Finally, what did you do to regulate your emotions? Write about how you transitioned from being shocked to how you were in the end.

The first few days might be a bit of a challenge but after that, you'll begin to notice how you're going to be mindful of your emotions and body language in any given situation.

This is a healthy exercise that is going to help you develop a deeper connection with yourself and help you identify the things that make you comfortable or uncomfortable.

From there, you'll begin to assert yourself as your feelings are going to force you to reconsider if you want to continue experiencing those kinds of feelings. Sure, you can't avoid getting bad news every once in a while, but you'll be able to work through the situations, such as when a disrespectful colleague or a rude family member humiliates you and makes you feel small. Your conscience will begin to highlight the fact that you cannot live like this and will drive you to make the necessary changes in your life.

In other cases, your emotional awareness may help you realize that sometimes you suppress your feelings even when they are valid.

How many times have you reflected on a situation and realized that you felt one way but reacted completely differently? Sometimes we're unhappy with a situation and we can't live on our true feelings because we're going to disappoint our friends or our families. This is not an enjoyable way to live and you'll thank yourself for working on correcting it.

The Power of Emotional Intelligence

A vast part of harnessing the power of being aware of your feelings is also about having the ability to assess and control our emotions, handle conflict, empathize with others, and communicate effectively. This is what we call emotional intelligence (EQ).

Emotional intelligence requires some level of authenticity and will allow you to grow and improve on your flaws. If you're wondering what separates an assertive woman from an unassertive woman, it's often one simple thing: a strong EQ!

Think about it, a woman who is aware of her feelings will be able to interpret them. If she can interpret them, not only will she be conscious of how they affect her, but she will also know how they affect the people around her.

You're probably wondering why other people should matter in this regard because they don't even respect your feelings, but that is one of the reasons why you should work on your EQ. You cannot claim to be emotionally intelligent if you're going to be ignoring other people's emotions. Allow yourself to be conscious of why people behave the way they do so that you can use that information to help you understand how you should communicate your needs or feelings to them.

For example, you have a colleague at work who always comes to you for help. You don't mind helping your friend out but you hate the fact that they spend so much time at your desk, and it's starting to affect your productivity. The problem is when your colleague comes to you for help, they don't check if you're available to help, they simply walk up to you and say "Can you help check this out for me, I'm so dumb; I keep on forgetting how done," or "I know you can do this for me, it's kinda urgent and you're my only hope." So yes, they make it obvious that you're doing them a favor but they also neglect to recognize the value of your time.

How would you react to this situation? If you're an aggressive woman you'll snap at the poor colleague and tell them to never come back to your desk again. As a passive woman, you'll try to maintain the peace by neglecting your work and then helping them anyway. As an assertive woman, you'll use your EQ to handle the situation.

Women with strong EQ will be:

- Empathetic: They relate with others on a basic human level.
- Solution-oriented: they know there's a problem, so they come up with a viable solution
- Effective communicators: Not only are they able to deliver a message transparently, but they are receptive and responsive too!
- Motivated: They have a positive spirit and a strong desire to do well.
- Leaders: They know how to take initiative and will not easily be influenced by what's the current 'in' thing.

Here is a guideline you can use in any situation to help you utilize your EQ.

1. Identify your emotion, thoughts, and the person's behavior.
2. Set healthy boundaries by inviting them to a conversation.
3. Express yourself by constructing a sentence that will start with "I" and contain all the elements that you've identified in step one.

Because you're an assertive woman, you can continue the steps and apply EQ by:

4. Listening to what they have to say. Perhaps you'll learn that they genuinely believe they're dumb because that's what they grew up being told, or that they struggle with remembering information due to a learning disability.
5. Show you're empathetic by thanking your colleague for opening up and then acknowledging their challenges.
6. Help them come up with a solution by suggesting that they should write down notes or a step-by-step guide on how to do the task you always help them out with. This shows you're a motivated person who is interested in finding solutions.
7. Show your leadership skills by following up every now and then, until they're comfortable with themselves.

Do you see how possible it is for you to end up in a win-win situation by asserting yourself? In the end, your colleague will thank you for handling this situation and you'll never have to worry about being behind with your work!

By now, you can see that you'll accomplish a few gentle steps toward being bold and courageous by simply identifying an emotion. Once you have done that, you can decide to never allow someone to make you feel like that again, or you could use it to spark an important and meaningful conversation.

Do you remember that in the beginning, we defined assertiveness as the ability to communicate your needs in a calm and respectful manner? This part of the chapter has illustrated how consistently working on your EQ will help you stay respectful and keep the peace.

Let's Talk About Body Language

There is no denying that your body language is highly dependent on your feelings. We often act based on how we feel. The problem kicks in when we communicate our feelings in an unsuitable manner.

Just as there is power in knowing your feelings and how others feel, you are going to learn that body language holds a similar weight. In fact, once you have learned to read other people's feelings, you are going to find it so much easier to be able to assert yourself. This is because body language is all about reflecting feelings back to the sender. For example, let's say you engage in a conversation with your friend and they begin to tell you about their problems. The most natural thing that you'll do is to immediately become compassionate and offer to hug them, hold their hands, or even use empathetic words. In any given situation, you should be able to behave in this exact manner, that is, receive cues and then act on them accordingly.

Because body language is not a universal dialect, we need to be cognizant of cultural, psychological, and developmental differences that might be open to interpretation. However, there are common gestures that you can incorporate in your life to show more courage and boldness.

Become Visible

When certain people walk into a room, people stop and notice them. There is something about the way they walk, how they're dressed, or even the way they interact with the environment that makes the world temporarily stop. On the other hand, some people walk into the room and no one notices them, life goes on and after a few minutes, they disappear as if they've never walked in at all.

How do people react when *you* walk into a room? You need not make grand entrances wherever you go but you should start thinking about allowing your body language to speak for you.

In any given environment, not only should people know that you exist, but they should also know that you are a woman who should be taken seriously. This doesn't mean that you should be loud, dress super flashy, or introduce yourself to everyone in the room. No, you simply need to start working on your appearance because it is what gives people hints about what you think of yourself.

Work on Your Presentation

We've all had an experience where we turned our heads and rolled our eyes when we saw a woman wearing an inappropriate outfit at a church service or in public. This type of reaction does not come from a judgmental place; it merely triggers us to make assumptions (which might be untrue) about her.

Now if we can make assumptions about a woman we've only seen once in our lives, imagine how many times you've been judged for the way you choose to appear to the public!

This brings us to a simple, yet powerful exercise that will lead to unbelievable results. Challenge yourself to start dressing up like an assertive woman. For a week, transform your wardrobe, hairstyle, and cleanliness. This exercise does not require you to change the way you look; it simply asks that you dress appropriately and strategically for the places you go.

To do this, you should:

- Apply more effort in your tidiness, even if you believe you have already made an effort. Make sure your hair is neat at all times, never for a second allow your lips to be dry, and if you wear makeup, make sure it's carefully applied.
- Dress appropriately for different occasions. If you work in an office, invest in more formal clothes that will make you comfortable. If you're going to go out with friends then buy a cute dress that will make you love your body a little more. Make people aware that you want to be wherever you're at.
- Focus on your hairstyle. You know the famous quote "A woman who cuts her hair is about to change her life." There is power in that statement and you should use it to your advantage. You don't even need to cut your hair, but you can change up your hairstyle every two days, or change the color to the one you've always wanted. Whatever it is, allow your hair to make you feel like your life is about to change!

Every day, write about how you felt when you looked at yourself in the mirror and how people noticed you when you walked into a room. This type of awareness is going to energize you so much that you won't stop dressing up after the seventh day!

Capitalize on Vocal Tone and Rhythm

Let's go back to 2014 when actress and activist Emma Watson delivered a powerful speech at the UN. She said, "I am from Britain. And I think it is right that I am paid the same as my male counterparts. I think it is right that I should be able to make decisions about my own body. I think it is right that socially I am afforded the same respect as men" (Sollosi, p. 1). She said this with conviction and confidence because she felt it was right to express herself and share her thoughts with the world. Many people believed her.

Now, imagine if she had said this with a low volume, stuttering, and adding "ahs" and "uhms" throughout her speech. That speech would've fallen flat and no one would've been moved by it. This proves that after feelings, the power of what you say is conveyed by how you say it.

As an assertive woman, your voice should always be pleasant and well presented for a situation. When you engage in an informal conversation, your volume should be skillfully controlled, and when you are in serious conversations that require you to be a bit firmer. Stand your ground by ensuring that your volume remains standard throughout.

In any conversation, an assertive woman aims to maintain a conversational flow and is careful not to stumble on her words. Even when she stumbles, she pauses, takes a deep breath, and then continues to make her point.

An Activity for Your Vocal Tone and Rhythm

Ask someone you trust to help you with this activity.

1. The partner you picked for this exercise should create a scenario that will require you to engage in a conversation. In this scenario, you should both be strangers to one another and your aim should be to get help from them. So, you could maybe be calling in to

get more information about their services, or you could be a customer who wants to complain about a product.
2. Once they reveal this scenario to you, give yourself about 10 minutes to rehearse how you're going to approach them. Don't focus on how the entire conversation might go, just think about how you're going to present the information to them.
3. When you are ready, initiate the conversation but allow your partner to lead the conversation. All you need to do is focus on the way you respond.
4. Remember to breathe! While your words are going to come from your head, your volume is highly dependent on your breathing. Ensure that you inhale from your diaphragm, exhale through your nose, and only speak as you are exhaling.
5. As you engage in this exercise, your partner should keep track of how many times you use words like "ah" and "uhm." They should also analyze the way you speak and how you control your breathing, volume, and rhythm. From there, they'll give you constructive feedback after the conversation.
6. From the feedback you receive, identify notable points that you should work on. Continue with this exercise for as long as you can and allow yourself to use these skills in real life.

The next time you're with your family and someone needs to make an order either on the phone or in person, take it upon yourself to place it. If you're prompted to engage with the store assistant the next time you do your shopping, quickly rehearse what you need to say, and then give yourself the courage to speak to them. You'll be surprised at how well it'll go with a little preparation!

Capitalize on Your Facial Expression and Posture

Your face has around 50 muscles that you can use to your advantage.

In order to appear calm and inviting, relax your forehead and keep your teeth slightly apart from each other. Maintain a solid smile and make eye contact that is occasionally broken by a quick look at another object or person.

Foster an optimistic posture by standing upright, with your face directly tilted to the person you're speaking to. Your shoulders should be held back and relaxed at all times. This will make you feel like you are in control of yourself in that particular environment and will also help you appear more confident.

An Activity for Your Body Language: Put on a Killer Act!

Have you ever dreamed of living your life as Naomi Campbell, Anna Wintour, or Nicola Sturgeon? Well, this fun exercise can give you that opportunity.

Think of a woman who you believe is the definition of assertiveness; it doesn't even have to be a celebrity. It could be your mother, friend, or colleague who you look up to at work.

Then follow these steps:
1. For a day, pretend that you are this powerful woman. You can even wear the type of accessories they like, or style your hair the way they usually do—anything to make you feel like you've inherited their power.

2. Pick a simple and safe place that you can go to on your own. Make sure it's an environment where you will be completely unknown and won't be at risk of bumping into someone you know and breaking character.
3. You have watched this woman speak and live her life with such a powerful force, and now it's your turn to experience what it's like to be that assertive. Let's say you chose to be your confident and outspoken aunt. She is known to visit art exhibitions and often sparks interesting conversations with the people she meets there.

   Maybe you don't have to start conversations, but you can walk in there as confidently as possible. Walk around and do what you think your aunt would do. If you happen to speak to someone, forget about the shy and unconfident woman that you left at home. You've acquired your aunt's confidence and this is your moment! Engage in the conversation, ask questions, and use positive body language to show your newfound acquaintance that you appreciate them talking to you.
4. When you're done, go back home and applaud yourself for stepping out of your comfort zone! Repeat this exercise as many times as you want until you step out of your house feeling like you no longer have to carry someone else's confidence to exist.

Good luck and have fun!

How to Use Body Language for Assertiveness in Challenging Situations

You've learned that the way you carry yourself speaks volumes, now it's time to use that to your advantage.

In this section, we are going to focus on difficult situations that require you to use your body language to put emphasis on the message you are trying to relay. When people know that we struggle with assertiveness, they often try to challenge us by getting louder, using emotional blackmail, and most importantly, utilizing the power of their body language.

Don't worry; that should no longer intimidate you because you are going to learn how to read their body language in order to rise to the challenge too!

Body Language in Difficult Conversations

Maybe you're trying to draw healthy boundaries or negotiate your working conditions. This type of situation is an emotionally charged one that requires you to use EQ to regulate your body language.

You could be calm and slightly nervous while you notice the other person tapping their feet, their arms folded, and showing little to no eye contact. From all of this you know they are emotional and indifferent, so the conversation might go south.

Great, you were able to read their body language so what are you going to do about it?

- You acknowledge how they feel but continue to stand your ground.
- When they speak, nod to show them that you're following what they're saying (and not necessarily agreeing with them).
- When you speak, you could also nod slowly in order to get them to notice you and think about what you're saying, especially if you're trying to get them to see your perspective.
- Ease off the tension and disarm an aggressive person by tilting your head slightly to the side, this shows that you are empathetic and are open to the discussion, no matter how hard it may be.

Once they are done talking, move your head back to its original position and then respond with another body language cue that will show that you are going to stand your ground. Research shows that if you maintain eye contact just 30% of the time during a conversation, people will remember what you say (Fullwood & Doherty-Sneddon, 2006).

So, look them straight in the eyes with a warm gaze, and then raise your point calmly.

- Use a considerable amount of hand gestures to make your points. People are more likely to remember what you're saying if they can attach it to a mental image. So, if you want to draw attention to how much their actions hurt you, you could hold your hand to your chest every time you use the word "hurt" or if you want to make them understand that there's only one thing that you want them to start doing, then show your pinky finger every time you tell them what you need from them.

Body Language for Interviews and Negotiations

The aim in scenarios like these is to show confidence in yourself and openness to the discussion.

- Maintain great posture by standing or sitting upright and placing your hands on the table or by your side. Remember, this shows that you're confident in yourself and are open to the discussion.
- Eye Contact: Make them remember what you're saying by giving a relaxing gaze for a few seconds, before finally resting your eyes on something else. Staring for too long makes you look creepy but making no eye contact makes you look untrustworthy, so don't go overboard!
- According to research, some people develop the habit of touching their face or playing with their hair whenever they tell a lie (Steinhilber, 2017). Avoid doing this in scenarios like these, especially if they've asked you a question.
- To build rapport, use mirroring to put the person you're in conversation with at ease.
- Hand gestures are very powerful in scenarios like this. Use them especially for descriptive words like 'move,' 'grow,' and 'calm.' This will make you and your interview even more memorable.

Although body language and emotions complement effective verbal communication, they are still not something you'll learn or master overnight.

To really benefit, you need to be aware of your current body language. Think of the many times you said something but your body screamed the opposite. Investigate why your body reacted the way it did. Which emotion caused you to react this way and how can you try to control it? For example, if you find yourself scratching your head every time someone makes a request that makes you uncomfortable, think of finding ways to consciously control this. The more you become aware of how your body reacts based on your emotions, the better you'll be equipped to handle it and send a more effective message to your recipients.

Chapter 6:

Let's Resolve Conflict and Communicate Instead

We cannot avoid conflict but how we resolve it is in our control. –Sabali Wanjiku

From the moment you started reading this book, you were driven by a deep desire to settle an uncomfortable battle within yourself. You knew what you wanted but kept on getting something else.

You struggled to resolve this even though this challenge drained you on so many levels. What you believed in as an individual did not match the life you were living, and that is what we call 'conflict.'

In its simplest form, conflict is a clash between two opposing ideas or people. You could clash with someone from work, a family member, your partner, and even yourself!

To conflict with something or someone can be a very disturbing and difficult thing. This is why people leave relationships, quit their jobs, and even end up being passive. They would rather try to avoid it than to face it head-on, and although it could be understandable why that is so, it is definitely not a viable option.

Why do we clash with people and ourselves? That is the million-dollar question. Is it because we don't gel well with certain personalities? Or that we expect too much from people and ourselves? The answer is quite simple, but as you have read throughout the book, I believe you'll understand why it's the foundation of it all.

When we dig deeper into what causes conflict, we realize that it all boils down to communication. We already know that as humans, we are all unique individuals with different expectations. The problem begins when another person doesn't meet or respect your expectations. By expectation, I mean that everyone carries a belief system that is often challenged, and when it reaches that point, we become emotional and start to question the other person's intentions.

Society has painted conflict as a negative thing because it often incites undesirable circumstances that are sometimes unhealthy for us. This is not always the case; it can sometimes be a good thing.

Yes, it can be positive. This is the reason why you're here after all. You have conflicted with yourself and have decided to use it for a better purpose. You are seeking better ways to become a more courageous and bolder woman.

Even in our relationships, we face conflict because we know there are better ways of approaching a situation or behaving.

In Comes Confrontation!

Conflict is something that does not like to walk alone. It is either followed by an unfair act of avoidance or it pushes you to a confrontation.

Confrontation is an important element of conflict that can make or break a relationship. It has also been painted out to be a negative thing because people expect it to be hostile and argumentative, but that is not always true. With careful planning and belief in yourself, you can create a win-win situation.

So, while conflict will make you realize there's an issue that needs to be addressed, confrontation helps you sort it out once and for all.

Can you guess what it is that will help you have a healthy confrontation? Yes, you guessed it—it's communication!

This chapter is going to help you identify the issue when you are in a conflicting situation and to communicate effectively when you are faced with a confrontation.

It All Starts With a Problem

Sometimes, you can't even prepare yourself for conflict because it happens so unexpectedly. However, there are times where an opposing idea lingers for so long that you are hardly surprised when it finally explodes.

The trick here is to identify the issue at hand. When you have a mild disagreement with someone or you find yourself uncomfortable because something clashes with your values or belief system, ask yourself what it is that is really bothering you.

Sometimes you could have an issue with someone, but other times you'll have a problem exclusively with their behavior. You must be able to differentiate the two.

For example, say you're clashing with your sister because she smokes, something that you believe she shouldn't be doing because of the health risks. While you are correct, it simply doesn't have anything to do with you. She doesn't smoke in the house, maintains good hygiene, and has never asked you to buy her cigarettes. This might sound like a simple issue, but most conflicts start like this. Before you know it, people are involved in heated arguments that go on forever.

On the other hand, you could still have the same problem but give a different reason. You know that she doesn't smoke in the house but you've caught her 'borrowing' a few notes from your bag because she was out of cigarettes. Now, that is enough to make you realize there is a real issue here. While you love her and have absolutely nothing against her, you don't appreciate the fact that she steals from you. That is the real problem that will have to be addressed.

So, how did we get to identifying the real issue in the situation? We had to figure out why it is a problem for you—it all comes down to you. If it makes you uncomfortable or clashes with what you believe in, then you've got an issue that is worth addressing.

How to Handle a Confrontation

In the next week, think of a situation that requires you to make an assertive request. It can be something as simple as asking your colleague to give you a deadline on when they'll submit the document you requested. Maybe you could ask your children to be more active with helping around the house, or you could request that your manager starts delegating some of your responsibilities to your other colleagues.

Now that you have an issue to solve, request a meeting with the person. Don't think of it as confrontation as that might trigger nervousness, but think of it as a discussion that will require you to communicate effectively using these steps:

1. Before the meeting, revert to the issue and think of how you're going to present it constructively. The most effective way of achieving this is to avoid reflecting on them as a problem. Instead, show them that you've got an issue with their behavior.
2. What is your desired outcome after the confrontation? Answer this question by stating the behavioral changes that you'd like to see. Your desired outcome is often driven by an overwhelming feeling. "I feel exploited because although I work hard, I believe I'm still underpaid" or "I feel unappreciated because even though I have worked hard to make this relationship work, it seems to be one-sided."

How to Make Requests and Communicate Effectively During the Confrontation

Before making your request, rehearse! Stand in front of the mirror and take special notice of your body language, your vocal tone, and your choice of words. Once you believe you are ready for the conversation, approach the person as boldly as you can.

Relax

Of course, you'll be nervous because you don't know what to expect, but the fact that you asked for an opportunity to speak about it means you are interested in a way forward and that's a bold move. Besides, your recipient has agreed to meet up with you, which indicates a willingness to hear you out.

As long as you rehearse your points, remain calm, and put yourself first, you'll be absolutely fine.

Consider Beginning With Small Talk

Make your recipient understand that you've got a specific problem with them and not with your overall relationship or them as individuals. One of the best ways you can achieve this is by thanking them for agreeing to meet with you and asking how they are. You could also extend your gratitude for them being in your life either as a loved one, colleague, or roommate. For example, you could say "Firstly, I appreciate the kind of relationship we've built over the years" or "I love how you've always been there for me throughout this journey." Anything that makes them realize that irrespective of the problems you have, you still appreciate them.

Pay Careful Attention to Body Language

Are you maintaining a calm voice? If you are, then be cognizant of the message you send across to the other person. Most importantly, take cues from how they use their body to tell you important messages, and then use that to your advantage.

Use the Deso Model to Start the Conversation

This is a four-step method designed by prominent behavioral and psychological experts Sharon and Gordon Bower that will help you communicate effectively. According to Researcher and Psychological expert Dr. Astray, "it is designed to help you raise your words, not your voice" (2020, para. 19).

One of the most beneficial things about using this model to design your script is that you won't over-explain yourself or downplay main points. It is going to help you get straight to the point in a clear and respectful manner.

Below are the four steps that comprise the model:

1. **Describe**

This step requires you to build a solid case by being specific about the issue at hand. It should be clear, behavioral, and focus on how it negatively affects you.

You should end up with something like "I have a problem with my sister stealing money from me to buy cigarettes" or "my children no longer do their chores, and it creates extra work for me."

So, for the example we made about your sister who smokes, you'll have a statement that reads, "I noticed that you've been taking money out of my purse to buy cigarettes."

2. Express

In this step, lay your case on the table by expressing how you feel about the situation. Claim your assertiveness by beginning your statement with "I" and remain calm, even if you start becoming emotional.

As you continue to express yourself, find ways to use positive words but be careful not to take advantage of the situation by exaggerating. So, instead of saying "I almost died when I caught you taking money from my purse," you could say "Although I respect that you smoke, I was disappointed when I caught you taking money from my purse."

3. Specify

Now that you have presented the problem, be proactive and introduce a solution. This is something that you would like to see the other person start doing.

Make sure your request is clear. "I'd appreciate it if you could start helping around the house with cleaning" is so much better than "Can you do your part at home?" This is your only chance to let the person know what exactly you need from them; use it wisely!

4. **Outcome**

In this final step, you demonstrate your assertiveness by letting the other person know what will happen if they respect or ignore your request. The payoff should preferably be positive but we know not all situations permit that. This ultimatum should be something that you have clearly thought about and are comfortable with.

There are various outcomes that you can settle on, but below are the four most common ones that can help determine what you really want.

- **Emotional**

If all you wanted to do was express yourself because it would make you feel better, then make it known to your recipient. In other cases, you know you'll feel better if they could work on their behavior; this is something that you should express to them as well.

"I'm so glad I could let it all out" or "I'd feel so much happier if you could help with…"

- **Rewarding**

In other circumstances, we are withholding a reward because we don't believe they deserve it yet. However, we believe that once they meet us halfway, we'll be willing to do something that we'd both like. Once you state your case, you can let them know that it won't go in vain. "Then I can maybe help with…" "I can lend you the car more," or "I'll handle the rest of the payment."

- **Concrete**

Sometimes, we call people out because we know they are capable of achieving excellent, tangible results. Think of a colleague who isn't being a team player or a partner who isn't bringing their A-game to the relationship. Sometimes all it takes is for another person to remind them of the benefits of changing their behavior.

"We'll be able to spend more time together" or "We'll get better results."

- **Punishable**

Sometimes people push our boundaries a little too much and that is totally unacceptable. For this outcome, you are not forcing them to do what you want; instead, you're demonstrating that bad behavior results in firm consequences, especially if their actions are selfish and hurtful. Maybe you'll end the relationship if your partner continues to be unfaithful to you or you'll report your sexist colleague to Human Resources if they continue to make you feel uncomfortable.

As for outcomes, you need to be very careful about how you present them and most importantly, carry them out. People are less likely to take you seriously if they notice that you don't stick to your word. This raises the chances of them continuing to take advantage of you.

In the end, people might resent you for putting your foot down and calling out their bad behavior, but that is what an assertive woman does. They stand their ground and remain unshaken in their quest to get what they desire in their lives.

Not only should you use this template to build a powerful argument, but you should also remember to stick to the point and avoid bringing up any other issues.

This means that even if your recipient attacks you, you'll remain calm and continue to raise your valid points. Furthermore, when they make valid points, let them know that their points are acknowledged and see what you can do with them.

Once you've used the DESO script to communicate your needs, continue to follow the steps below:

Resolve It

Some call it finding a common ground, while others refer to it as compromising, but you and your recipient should be able to resolve the issue at hand. Throughout the conversation, you might find that the issue wasn't as hectic as you thought it was, and after you start looking at it from the other person's perspective, you might find that there are a few things that you can both do that will help your relationship and solve the issue at hand.

Be Open to an Unknown Outcome

When we go into a confrontation, we often imagine how the conversation will end. We wish for the other person to forgive and tell us that they'll never upset us again, or we anticipate rejection and termination of our relationship. This kind of mentality is only going to set you up for disappointment.

Tell yourself that you are open to any kind of conclusion, as long as you'll walk away having said what you needed to.

Furthermore, remember that any kind of outcome has a possibility of a way forward, even if it's not the one that you anticipated.

After the Confrontation

Wow, so you've finally gained the courage to speak about a matter that has been a challenge in your life. You've now settled into either a win-win environment, or you've walked away having made someone upset and in complete disbelief of your boldness. Whatever the case is, pat yourself on the shoulder for making such a daring move!

No matter how tempting it'll be, don't feel guilty for speaking up about your needs; you deserve to get exactly what feels right for you.

Depending on the outcome of the confrontation, decide whether you are willing to move forward with this person or not. If you are, and they are also open to a second chance, monitor any changes that occur. Embrace them if you are satisfied, and consider finding another solution if you are not. It's your feelings that are a priority here, so as long as you feel good, then all will be good.

Most women are scared to make requests because they think it makes them look controlling and they fear living with the consequences of what might happen.

In reality, though, requests, discussions, and confrontations are designed to help us state our needs and what we'd like to see happen. We are informing others of our desires. We leave it up to them to decide whether they will go along with the request. However, the most important thing is that you gain the courage to let people know that there is a specific life you'd like to live, and they should adjust their behavior if they value you.

Conclusion

Congratulations! Can you believe you've made it this far?

From the moment you started reading this book, you knew you had the potential to be assertive; it was just a matter of finding the right guidelines to set you up for success.

Assertiveness is more than just a skill; it's a decision that you choose to make every day of your life. When it challenges you to move out of your comfort zone, it demands that you do it correctly; otherwise, you'll never break the cycle of being taken advantage of.

It asks the right questions and demands honest answers, irrespective of whether you're confident or struggling with your self-esteem. What do you want to happen in your life? How does this situation make you feel, and most importantly, what are you going to do about it?

Because assertiveness is an internal process, allow yourself to work on your inner challenges even on days when it doesn't feel like it's worth it. Gradually, it will begin to show itself externally and the people around you will notice it too.

All of the activities shared in this book are easy to follow, effective, and fun to do. While you work on them, trust them to reveal honest points about yourself that you should work on, and I promise you that you'll get the results you've always wanted.

Now that you're equipped with powerful tools to help you transform your life and become the assertive woman that you've always wanted to be, embrace the journey and make sure you enjoy it!

Each morning, you should challenge yourself to put yourself first. Be intentional about it in the way you walk, talk, and present yourself to the world because that is the strongest message you can put out there about yourself.

As you begin to think of all the changes you need to make in your life, remind yourself that you should take things one step at a time until you finally reach your desired destination. Of course, it's going to be frustrating at first, but the world requires more assertive women. Besides that, you need to be gentle with yourself; remember, it all starts with you.

This is the time for you to fall in love with yourself again. Take in your strengths, weaknesses, and flaws, and embrace them! Prove that you want to put yourself first by saying "I" and "no" more often, with a stern attitude, a gentle smile, and an assertive voice.

There are so many effective guidelines inside this book that are going to help in any situation that you'll encounter in life; it's up to you to practice until you are confident enough to get what you want. Some exercises might seem a bit too extreme for you in the beginning; it's okay to skip them, as long as you promise yourself to practice them as soon as you're ready.

As you continue in this journey of assertiveness, trust that your journal will teach you powerful things about yourself that you never knew existed. Keep it in a safe place, and know that it will help you succeed.

When you reach the point where you have to draw boundaries, think of the imaginary line that nobody should cross. Remember that you've got the right to have and own your personal space. Why should anyone cross it if you are so careful not to cross their boundaries?

I'm not going to lie and tell you that this is the type of book that requires you to only read it once and then you'll be set for life. No, you're going to have to make it your best friend. Whether you're in doubt or need a reminder on how to love yourself again, repetition is key. Capitalize on your knowledge of body language to create a win-win situation, and refer back to it as many times as needed.

From today, trust your body to speak assertive language. Take conflict, confrontation, boundaries, limitations, and constructive criticism as an opportunity for you to grow. No more putting other people first, being passive, or unnecessarily aggressive. This is your time to live up to the values you've set for yourself.

Once again, congratulations on becoming a brave and courageous woman, it looks good on you!

References

Amanatullah, E. T., & Morris, M. W. (2020). *Negotiating gender roles: gender differences in assertive negotiating are mediated by women's fear of backlash and attenuated when negotiating on behalf of others | Gender Action Portal*. Harvard.edu. https://gap.hks.harvard.edu/negotiating-gender-roles-gender-differences-assertive-negotiating-are-mediated-women%E2%80%99s-fear-backlash

Barroso, A., & Brown, A. (2021, May 25). *Gender pay gap in U.S. held steady in 2020*. Pew Research Center. https://www.pewresearch.org/fact-tank/2021/05/25/gender-pay-gap-facts/

Bloch, R. (2015, October 10). *"What you do speaks so loudly I cannot hear what you are saying."* Medium. https://medium.com/golden-eggs/what-you-do-speaks-so-loudly-i-cannot-hear-what-you-are-saying-92fbfdf52472

Bolton, R. (1986). *People skills*. Simon & Schuster Inc.

Brand Minds. (2019, May 3). *Are women less assertive than men in the workplace?* Medium. https://brand-minds.medium.com/are-women-less-assertive-than-men-in-the-workplace-5faf138963ce

Cascio, C. N., O'Donnell, M. B., Tinney, F. J., Lieberman, M. D., Taylor, S. E., Strecher, V. J., & Falk, E. B. (2015). *Self-affirmation activates brain systems associated with self-related*

111

processing and reward and is reinforced by future orientation. Social Cognitive and Affective Neuroscience, 11(4), 621–629. https://doi.org/10.1093/scan/nsv136

Clarke, R. (2021, November 26). *"No one can make you feel inferior without your consent."* ~ Eleanor Roosevelt. ILLUMINATION-Curated. https://medium.com/illumination-curated/no-one-can-make-you-feel-inferior-without-your-consent-eleanor-roosevelt-842e552e52c6

Contributor, M. F. (2019, September 13). *Self-made millionaire: The simple strategy that helped increase my odds of success by 42%.* CNBC. https://www.cnbc.com/2019/09/13/self-made-millionaire-how-to-increase-your-odds-of-success-by-42-percent-marie-forleo.html

Corporate finance institute. (2015). *SMART Goal - Definition, guide, and importance of goal setting.* Corporate Finance Institute. https://corporatefinanceinstitute.com/resources/knowledge/other/smart-goal/

Davenport, B. (2014). *Building confidence: your guide to get motivated, be assertive, conquer fear, and empower your life for success.* Bold Living Press.

Dr. Astray, T. (2020, March 19). *Communication tool: Assertive confrontation and boundary setting with the DESO Script.* Dr. Astray. http://www.tatianaastray.com/managing-relationships/2020/3/18/communication-tool-assertive-confrontation-and-boundary-setting-with-the-deso-script

Economy, P. (2018, February 28). *This is the way you need to write down your goals for faster success*. Inc.com. https://www.inc.com/peter-economy/this-is-way-you-need-to-write-down-your-goals-for-faster-success.html#:~:text=Psychology%20professor%20Dr.

Freedman, J. (2019, October 24). *Women say sorry 295,650 times in their lives – and something needs to change*. www.tyla.com. https://www.tyla.com/news/life-news-women-say-sorry-more-men-295650-times-statistics-stop-apologise-20191024

Fullwood, C., & Doherty-Sneddon, G. (2006). *Effect of gazing at the camera during a video link on recall*. Applied ergonomics, 37(2), 167–175. https://doi.org/10.1016/j.apergo.2005.05.003

Garvey, M. (n.d.). *A quote by Marcus Garvey*. www.goodreads.com. Retrieved January 5, 2022, from https://www.goodreads.com/quotes/108316-if-you-haven-t-confidence-in-self-you-are-twice-defeated

Hagi, S. (2016, November 28). *It pays to be an assertive woman in the workplace, new study says*. www.vice.com. https://www.vice.com/en/article/qvdpnb/it-pays-to-be-an-assertive-woman-in-the-workplace-new-study-says

Hollandsworth, J. G., & Wall, K. E. (1977). *APA PsycNet*. Psycnet.apa.org. https://psycnet.apa.org/record/1977-29579-001

Idlehearts. (n.d.). *I encourage people to remember that "no" is a complete sentence*. IdleHearts. Retrieved January 5, 2022, from https://www.idlehearts.com/1805701/i-encourage-people-to-remember-that-no-is-a-complete-sentence

Julie De Azevedo-Hanks. (2016). *The assertiveness guide for women : how to communicate your needs, set healthy boundaries, & transform your relationships.* New Harbinger Publications.

Kim, J. (2016, March 29). *Why women can't accept compliments | Psychology Today South Africa.* www.psychologytoday.com. https://www.psychologytoday.com/za/blog/valley-girl-brain/201603/why-women-cant-accept-compliments

Kruse, K. (n.d.). *Get outside your comfort zone: how to tackle your fear.* Forbes. https://www.forbes.com/sites/kevinkruse/2017/06/13/get-outside-your-comfort-zone-how-to-tackle-your-fear/?sh=135f25297b59

Maccoby, E. E. (2000). *Parenting and its effects on children: on reading and misreading behavior genetics.* Annual Review of Psychology, 51(1), 1–27. https://doi.org/10.1146/annurev.psych.51.1.1

Martin, S. (2018, April 24). *what are boundaries and why do I need them?* Live Well with Sharon Martin. https://www.livewellwithsharonmartin.com/what-are-boundaries/

Masterclass Staff. (2020, November 8). *How to use the 7-38-55 rule to negotiate effectively.* https://www.masterclass.com/articles/how-to-use-the-7-38-55-rule-to-negotiate-effectively

McConchie, R. (n.d.). *Being assertive and proactive | Women in Research | Australia*. Women in Research. https://www.womeninresearch.org.au/being-assertive-and-proactive

MindTools. (2009). *Body languagepicking up and understanding nonverbal signals*. Mindtools.com. https://www.mindtools.com/pages/article/Body_Language.htm

Morin, A. (2019, January 2). *Women only accept compliments 40 percent of the time (but that number is even lower when the compliment comes from this group)*. Inc.com. https://www.inc.com/amy-morin/how-mentally-strong-women-respond-to-compliments.html

Park, A. (2018, August 10). *Issa Rae shares advice from Shonda Rhimes and Ava DuVernay on "The Late Show."* www.cbsnews.com. https://www.cbsnews.com/news/issa-rae-shares-advice-from-shonda-rhimes-ava-duvernay-on-the-late-show/

Paterson, R. J. (2000). *Assertiveness workbook how to express your ideas and stand up for yourself*. New Harbinger Publications, U.S.

Rabbitt, M. (2015, April 23). *Ohhh, So this is why so many women can't take a compliment*. Women's Health. https://www.womenshealthmag.com/life/a19914367/how-to-accept-a-compliment/

Raypole, C. (2020, January 15). *Body Language: What it is and how to read it*. Healthline. https://www.healthline.com/health/body-language

115

Sollosi, M. (2021, March 8). *12 of Emma Watson's most powerful quotes about feminism*. EW.com. https://ew.com/movies/2017/03/01/emma-watson-feminism-quotes/

Staff, G. (2015, April 14). *How women undermine themselves with words*. Goop. https://goop.com/wellness/career-money/how-women-undermine-themselves-with-words/

Steinhilber, B. (2018, August 20). *How to tell if someone is lying to you, according to researchers*. NBC News; NBC News. https://www.nbcnews.com/better/health/how-tell-if-someone-lying-according-behavioral-experts-ncna786326

The Resilience Lab. (n.d.). *Boundaries! OTR*. Retrieved January 5, 2022, from https://www.otrbristol.org.uk/the-resilience-lab/tips-tricks/boundaries/

Wanjiku, S. (2020, January 13). *Conflict Resolution: The healthy way*. Sabaliwanjiku.com. https://sabaliwanjiku.wixsite.com/website/post/conflict-resolution-the-healthy-way

Watson, E. (n.d.). *Emma Watson Speech*. UN Event.

Printed in Great Britain
by Amazon